Working Together for Local Integration of Migrants and Refugees in Vienna

This document, as well as any data and any map included herein, are without prejudice to the status of or sovereignty over any territory, to the delimitation of international frontiers and boundaries and to the name of any territory, city or area.

Please cite this publication as:
OECD (2018), *Working Together for Local Integration of Migrants and Refugees in Vienna*, OECD Publishing, Paris.
https://doi.org/10.1787/9789264304147-en

ISBN 978-92-64-30413-0 (print)
ISBN 978-92-64-30414-7 (PDF)

The statistical data for Israel are supplied by and under the responsibility of the relevant Israeli authorities. The use of such data by the OECD is without prejudice to the status of the Golan Heights, East Jerusalem and Israeli settlements in the West Bank under the terms of international law.

Photo credits: Cover © Marianne Colombani

Foreword

An OECD-EU initiative: "Territorial approach to migrant integration: The role of local authorities"

This publication *Migrant Integration in Vienna* was produced by the OECD as part of a larger study, *Territorial Approach to Migrant Integration: The Role of Local Authorities*, with the support of the European Commission.

The study takes stock of the existing multi-level governance frameworks and policies for migrant and refugee integration at the local level in nine large European cities: Amsterdam, Athens, Barcelona, Berlin, Glasgow, Gothenburg, Paris, Rome and Vienna and the small city case of Altena. It also builds on information collected from other 61 European cities through an ad hoc survey thanks to the partnership with the Council of European Municipalities and Regions (CEMR) and Eurocities and on a statistical database on migrant outcomes at regional (TL2) level. This study resulted in the report, ***Working Together for Local Integration of Migrants and Refugees***, approved by the OECD Committee for Regional Development Policy (RDPC) in December 2017 (OECD, 2018).

The focus of this study is on ''migrants' integration'', meaning a wide range of different groups of people with different reasons for leaving their countries of origin: humanitarian, economic, family or study, among others. The target group includes newcomers as well as migrants who settled in the cities many years ago and native-born people with at least one migrant parent,[1] depending on the statistical definition used by the city/country. Given the recent increase in the arrival of refugees and asylum seekers in Europe, particular attention is paid to these groups throughout the case studies.

Cities in the sample have different track records in integrating migrants. The study looks at updates to the governance mechanisms in the wake of the recent influx of asylum seekers and refugees, in order to improve the local reception of migrants and the capacity to integrate them into society. Conversely, it also investigates opportunities to extend some of the services recently established for newcomers to long-standing migrant groups.

The point of departure for the overall study is the observation that in practice integration takes place at the local level and should benefit both migrant and host communities through appropriate local development strategies. Cities are focal spots of refugee and migrant reception and integration processes: in 2015, close to two-thirds of the foreign-born population in the OECD lived in urban areas (OECD, 2018). However it seems that asylum seekers, at least in Europe, are more equally spread across regions. This new situation required responses from previously uninvolved cities and regions, in particular, in smaller-sized cities and non-urban regions. Following, the question of linking migrant

---

1.   Please refer to the definition of migration provided below.

integration policies with regional development policies emerged for sub-national governments.

The ambition of this series of case studies is to identify *how* cities have responded to these objectives. It aims to address an information vacuum: beyond the dominant literature on international and national evidence about migrant movements and integration, several studies exist about the local dimension and impact of migration without converging towards general results.[2] In addition, they just partially explore the governance factor attached to it. In the view of partner cities and international organisations (United Nations High Commissioner for Refugees [UNHCR], etc.), multi-level governance can be an important explanatory factor of the performance of migrant integration policies. Even though migration policies are the responsibility of the national government, the concentration of migrants in cities, and particularly in metropolitan areas (Boulant, J., M. Brezzi and P. Veneri, 2016; Diaz Ramirez, Liebig, Thoreau and Veneri, 2018), has an impact on the local demand for work, housing, goods and services that local authorities have to manage. Local authorities act within a multi-level budgetary and administrative framework, which limits or adds responsibilities in dealing with migrant-specific impacts in their territory. As such, this work first aims at understanding the way cities and their partners address migrant integration issues. While it doesn't strive at this stage to evaluate the impact of the whole set of local public actions, it compiles qualitative evidence of city policies across selected multi-level governance dimensions. These dimensions were selected according to the multi-level governance gaps analysis developed by the OECD (Charbit, 2011; Charbit and Michalun, 2009). Statistical data have been collected from all of the cities on the presence and outcomes of migrant and refugee populations.

As a result of this comparative work, and in collaboration with the partner cities and organisations, the OECD has compiled a list of key objectives to guide policy makers integrating migrants with a multi-governance perspective. The ***Checklist for Public Action to Migrant Integration at the Local Level*** is articulated according to 4 blocks and 12 objectives. The four blocks cover: 1) institutional and financial settings; 2) time and proximity as keys for migrants and host communities to live together; 3) enabling conditions for policy formulation and implementation; and 4) sectoral policies related to integration: access to the labour market, housing, social welfare and health, and education (see the checklist in Part II).

This study first provides insight on the city's migration background and current situation. It then provides a description of the actions implemented following the framework of the *Checklist for Public Action to Migrant Integration at the Local Level*.

The objective is to allow cities to learn from each other and to provide national and supranational decision makers and key partners of local integration policies with better evidence to address the major challenges ahead in this field and to adopt appropriate incentive schemes.

---

2.   Refer to the bibliography of the Synthesis Report.

Acknowledgements

This publication, *Working Together for Local Integration of Migrants and Refugees: The Case of Vienna*, was produced by the OECD in partnership with the European Commission as part of a larger study on "Territorial Approach to Migrant Integration: The Role of Local Authorities".

This case study has been initially written by Ursula Reeger (Institute for Urban and Regional research/Austrian Academy of Sciences), under the supervision of Claire Charbit, Head of the Territorial Dialogues and Migration Unit, within the Centre for Entrepreneurship, SMEs, Regions and Cities of the OECD. This report is based on substantive additional inputs and contributions from Anna Piccinni (OECD) and Lisanne Raderschall (OECD).

The case study has been carried out thanks to the close collaboration of the Municipality of Vienna who provided the information and organised the OECD field work. The OECD Secretariat would like to express its gratitude to all the participants at the interviews (see Annex A), and in particular the national government representatives and the staff of the municipality, with special thanks to Theodora Manolakos, Karin Konig and Ursula Struppe for their continuous support throughout the case study. The OECD Secretariat would also like to thank Johannes Gielge (Head of Unit Research Urban Planning) for his participation in this work.

This case study benefitted from comments from other colleagues across OECD directorates: in particular from Thomas Liebig, International Migration Division of the Directorate for Employment, Labor and Social Affairs.

The OECD Secretariat is especially thankful for the financial contribution and the collaboration throughout the implementation of the project with the European Union Directorate General for Regional and Urban Policy. In particular, we would like to thank Andor Urmos and Louise Bonneau for their guidance as well as for their substantive inputs during the revision of the case study.

Table of contents

Tables

Figures

Boxes

Abbreviations and acronyms

Acronym	German	English
AK Wien/ Vienna	Arbeitskammer	Chamber of Labour
AMS	Arbeitsmarktservice Wien	Public Employment Services
AST	Anlaufstelle für Personen mit im Ausland erworbenen Qualifikationen	Contact Points for the Recognition and Assessment of Qualifications Obtained Abroad
BEIMA	Bundesministerium Europa Integration Ausseres	Federal Ministry Europe Integration Foreign Affairs
BFA	Bundesamt für Fremdwesen und Asyl	Federal Office for Immigration and Asylum
BMASK	Bundessozialministerium	Federal Ministry of Labour, Social Affairs and Consumer Protection
BMI	Bundesministerium für Inneres	Ministry of Interior
BMS	Bedarfsorientierte Mindestsicherung BMS	Needs-based minimum income
FSW	Fond Soziales Wien	Vienna Social Welfare Fund
MA 17	Magistratsabteilung 17 Integration und Diversität	Integration and Diversity
MA 18	Magistratsabteilung 18Stadtentwicklung und Stadtplanung	Urban Development and Planning
MA 23	Magistratsabteilung Wirtschaft, Arbeit und Statistik	Economic Affairs, Labour and Statistics
MA 24	Magistratsabteilung Sozial und Gesundheitsplanung	Health Care and Social Welfare Planning
MA 35	Magistratsabteilung	Immigration and Citizenship
ÖIF	Österreichischer Integration Trust	Austrian Integration Fund
ÖSD	Österreichisches Sprach Diplom	Austrian language diploma
NAP.I	Nationaler Aktionsplan Integration	National Action Plan for Integration
UNDOK	Allaufstelle zur gewerkschaftlichen Unterstützung UNDOKumentiert Arbeitender	Contact point union support for undocumented workers
WAFF	Wiener Arbeitnehmer und Förderung Fonds	Vienna Employment Promotion Fund
WK Wien/ Vienna	Wirtschaftskammer	Chamber of Economics
WKOE	Österreichische Wirtschaftskammern	Austrian Economic Chamber
WWH	Verband Wiener Wohnungslosenhilfe	Viennese Assistance to the Homeless

Executive summary

Vienna is a fast-growing city that will most probably cross the 2-million-inhabitants threshold before 2030. Its population growth has been positive ever since the millennium and is largely related to immigration from abroad. In 2016, net migration to Vienna amounted to 22 000 persons. Overall, 35% (or 704 902 people) of Vienna's total population of 1 840 226 people, were born abroad and 50% have a migration background.[1] Some 61% of migrants have been in Vienna for more than ten years. Among the whole population, foreign-born individuals from third countries[2] represent the largest group with a share of 22.8%; EU/EFTA country nationals make up 15.5% of the population. Foreign-born individuals from Serbia (5.4%) and Turkey (4.1%) constitute the largest population share, while Germans represent the third largest group (3%). Furthermore, since 2015, the number of asylum seekers and refugees in the city has increased sharply. Vienna currently hosts 20 500 people in need of basic assistance, 15 000 more than in 2011; most of these are asylum seekers.[3]

Historically, actions to address migrant needs were first initiated at the local level in Austria. Vienna, characterised by increasing migrant numbers for a long time, has learned to accommodate this development also in its administrative structures and local policies. From 1971 onwards the city started having municipal institutions dedicated to the integration of migrants and refugees providing counselling in legal and social issues, language courses, school preparation programmes and healthcare advice, under the name of the "Migrants Fund" (*Zuwanderer-Fonds*) and later, the "Fund for Integration". Today, Vienna has defined its own local integration concept, and institutionalised integration and diversity into policy making. These engagements are oversight by the Municipal Department for Integration and Diversity (MA 17) which leads integration mainstreaming across public policies through dialogue with internal and external stakeholders and providing training. Most importantly since ten years this department monitors integration results by producing the Integration and Diversity Monitoring Report of the City of Vienna.

As a federal province[4] Vienna has additional competences compared to a city, it can directly negotiate agreements with the federal government. Some of these agreements have direct implications for migrants. For instance a recent agreement between the state and the provinces made compulsory kindergarten for all children for one year, including migrant kids, with important consequences for their early language integration.

The main aim of this case study is to reflect upon and analyse how the city of Vienna organises and implements integration and reception measures for migrants and refugees across levels of government, across city departments, as well as in interaction with other local stakeholders.

Key findings

This report presents key findings according to the *Checklist for Public Action to Migrant Integration at the Local Level.* Some of the remaining challenges, accomplishments and potential improvements are summarised here.

Some of the remaining challenges

Integration into the labour market

Data collected through the Integration and Diversity Monitoring of the city of Vienna (City of Vienna 2014, 102) highlight the significant gaps in labour market inclusion between Austrian and non-Austrian citizens as well as between Austrian with a foreign education or training certificate. In Vienna, third-countries migrants not educated in Austria have 11 percentage points difference in employment rate than those born abroad, but trained in the country of residence. Further foreign-born people educated abroad run a greater risk of being employed in poorly paid positions despite intermediate or higher education. In Vienna, persons with foreign diplomas frequently occupy positions below those of Austrians with similar qualifications. Currently, 56% of foreign persons in employment holding higher education qualifications from third countries are employed as unskilled or semi-skilled workers. In order to especially target unemployment of young people who have not had any schooling, regardless of their origins, the city and other important stakeholders such as the Trade Union and the Public Employment Service have collaboratively set up the "Vienna Qualification Plan" (Chapter 6). The plan aims to close the gap between low-qualified people and a labour market that requires well-qualified staff. Migrants are over-represented among youth with low qualifications thus this plan might have a strong impact on integration.

Education

To complement federal policies and initiatives for the recognition of qualification obtained abroad, the city offers counselling as part of the city's integration programme "Start Wien" to guide migrants through the process of recognition. Further, the Vienna Board of Education has established transitional classes with the aim of harmonising education levels reached abroad with Austrian standards so as to facilitate the possibility to continue education in Austria and obtaining Austrian qualification.

Additional multi-lingual resources and training for teachers are necessary to ensure the successful integration of migrant children in schools. Challenges resulting from the growing diversity of the Vienna population further require an increase of educational facilities and staff for migrant pupils in schools and for adults. As part of the city's responsibility concerning social inclusion policies for youth, Vienna offers options for the education of pupils beyond mandatory schooling age. These so-called "youth colleges" fill gaps in educational provision. Language courses in Austria are not structured in a coherent system. As there is a great variety and diversity among language course providers, the situation is often non-transparent for migrants and refugees who struggle to find courses that fit their needs and are of good quality. To address this, the city of Vienna has established a database of all courses, and advises migrants in coaching sessions that are part of the municipal welcome programme "Start Wien", on which course fits their individual needs. For asylum seekers, the city has introduced a tool that ensures placement into available courses funded by the city.

What is already accomplished and how could it be improved?

Policy coherence and co-operation

A National Action Plan for Integration (NAP.I) was agreed on in 2010 with the aim of pooling all integration policies existing at local level (Vienna had one since 1971) and ensuring co-operation across levels of government. This is an important mechanism to structure co-operation better and build coherent policies. Important steps to improve implementation of this mechanism have been to set up co-ordinating structures on integration based on dialogue with different levels of government. They have been developed since 2010 (i.e. Advisory Board on Integration). Vienna's dual position, as a city and a province, provides the administration with the ability to engage with the federal level from two standpoints, giving it greater access to decision-making processes than other cities have.

Evaluation and capacity building

The establishment of MA 17 institutionalised diversity and integration management as a central topic within the city administration. It helps to promote intercultural competences and sensibility across all sectors of the administration and further monitors other departments' work in incorporating integration-sensitive approaches. For instance, it published a guideline to implement diversity management and offers training and seminars on intercultural and integration issues.

Vienna has established very developed evaluation mechanisms for measuring migrant integration. Produced every two years since 2010, the integration evaluation framework of Vienna, the *Weiner Integrations- & Diversitätsmonitor*, is a holistic approach that encourages constant reviewing of the current policies. This includes analysing how politics and administration (43 departments and institutions are monitored) are meeting the needs of its diverse population and monitoring developments over time. In its last analysis in 2017, it observed a positive tendency with a rising number of departments offering multi-lingual services as well as embedding diversity management in their strategic priorities. It also found that shares of employees of foreign origin in city's management positions, and among youth, were still fairly low.

On the downside, evaluations of the individual projects the city undertakes, such as "Start Wien" do not take place comprehensively; thus it is difficult to assess their specific impact on integration dynamics. Also, it remains unclear how far the results of the monitoring are used to adapt policy making according to the evidence generated. To enhance the effectiveness of the monitoring and to benefit from the data collected, a structured feedback mechanism to policy making could be beneficial.

Participation and consultative methods

Vienna has no institutionalised measures for the participation of migrants in the city's political life and is lacking a permanent co-ordination platform with non-governmental organisations (NGOs) on strategic integration questions since the Vienna Integration Conference was abolished in 2009. However, MA 17 largely engages in informal communication with more than 400 migrant associations, organising meetings at the district or city level covering specific topics. Further, major projects (e.g. Start Wien) and the evolvement of the local integration concepts are developed in consultation with the respective communities. Adding to these consultations, more formalised representation could make sure migrants' needs are not overlooked.

Good practices that could be replicated

Starting integration from Day 1

Vienna's ambition is that integration measures start from the first day of arrival. The city has created a one-stop called "Start Wien" to facilitate the settling process of newly arrived migrants, refugees and asylum seekers. It functions as a comprehensive information and coaching programme combining counselling and information modules on administrative processes as well as city life, with advice for language courses. According to the migrant's legal status and needs, a personal integration trajectory is designed, carefully drawing on the migrant's past experiences and skills. This for example involves a competency check. For young asylum seekers, recognised refugees and migrants beyond compulsory school age (15-21), the programme includes a "youth college" aiming to qualify youth for entering into secondary schools or vocational training. Asylum seekers were recently included among the beneficiaries of these services, acknowledging the need to start integration as early as possible and use the time they have while awaiting asylum decisions. However, StartWien is explicitly designed for people who have resided in Vienna for less than two years. All others are not eligible to benefit from the approach of StartWien and have to rely on other measures.

Enhancing proximity by creating spaces where interaction brings migrant and native-born communities closer

Compared to other cities analysed, segregation is less of a problem in Vienna, as migrants usually have access to social housing after a certain time living in the city and are largely represented in the private housing market thus dispersed across the city. The municipal administration is very engaged in highlighting the added value of migration for the city and building proximity between different groups. On this note, the city facilitated the creation of the "Vienna Charter", a document that defines a framework for good neighbourhood relations, developed through a unique public participation process open to everyone. It involved 8 500 participants of different backgrounds and 12 700 hours of discussions. Further, "Wohnpartner", has been established to promote peaceful cohabitation and prevent neighbourhood conflict. Contact points are available in 22 locations in Vienna to assist when conflicts arise and support community work within social housing. In order to also reach migrants, the service employed people who speak 23 different languages.

Notes

1. Citizens holding Austrian citizenship who have a migration background are persons who have at least one parent that was born abroad or holds foreign nationalities. These will also be referred to as native-born children of migrant parents.

2. Non- EU/EFTA.

3. In Austria, asylum seekers are among the group of foreigners who receive so-called "basic assistance". There is an agreement between the federal state of Austria and the federal provinces about support provided to foreigners in need of protection called "Grundversorgungsvereinbarung - Art. 15a B-VG". Target groups are people who have applied for asylum and await the decision, those have not been granted asylum but cannot return to their countries of origin, as well as those who were granted asylum for the first four months after recognition.

4.   The term "federal provinces" is used here as a generic term to refer to the constituent regions of a federation. They have specific names depending on the federation: states or provinces in Austria (*Bundesländer*). In Austria's federal system, provinces have their own legislative bodies, executive organs and financial management. Certain legislative matters are also reserved for the provinces.

Key data on migrant presence and integration in Vienna

Figure 1. Vienna's location in Austria according to the OECD regional classification

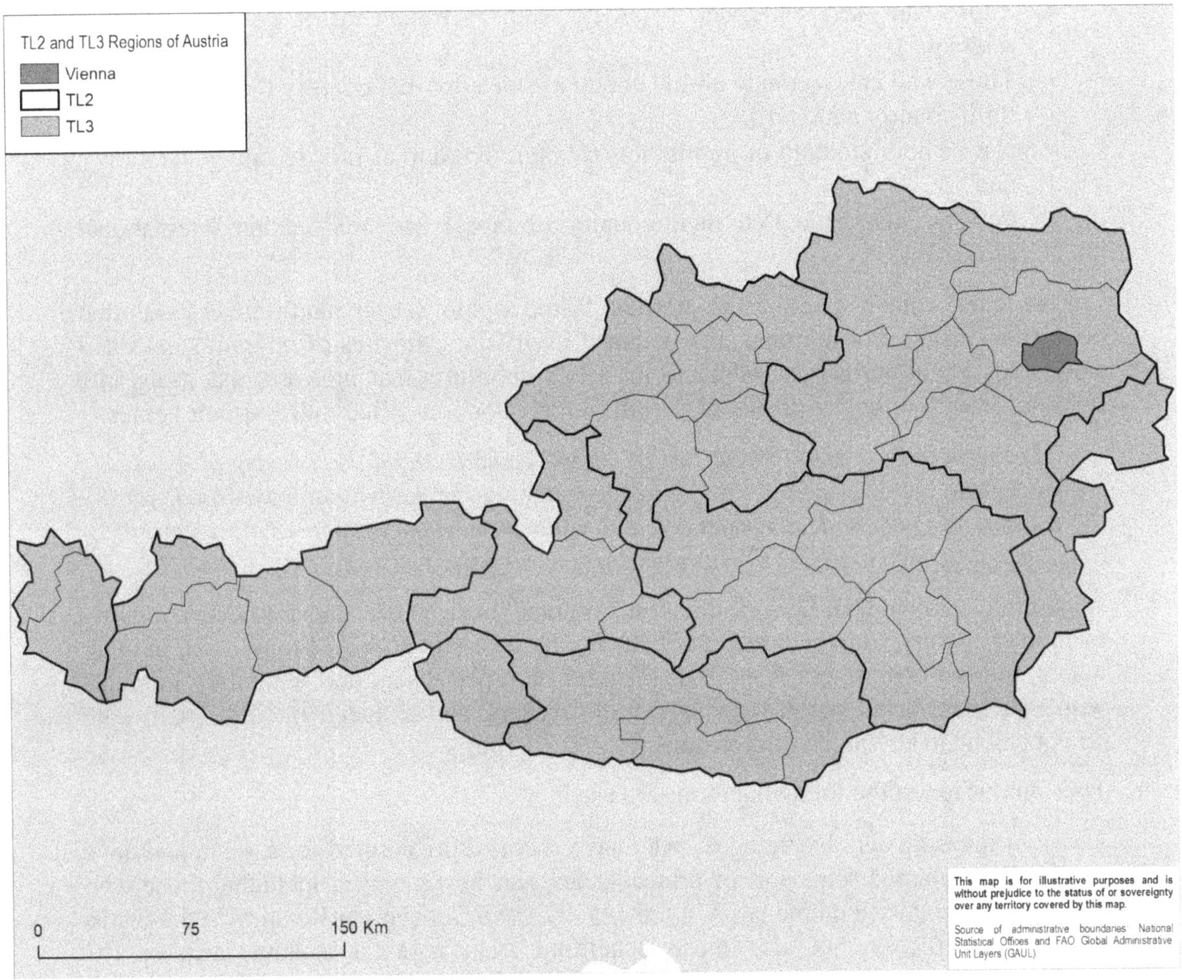

Note: TL2: Territorial Level 2 consists of the OECD classification of regions within each member country. There are 335 regions classified at this level across 35 member countries. Austria has 9 TL2 level regions. TL3: Territorial Level 3 consists of the lower level of classification and is composed of 1 681 small regions. In most cases, they correspond to administrative regions. Austria has 35 TL level small regions.
Source: OECD (2018), *OECD Regional Statistics Database*, http://dx.doi.org/10.1787/region-data-en.

Definition of migration

The term "migrant" generally functions as an umbrella term used to describe people that move to another country with the intention of staying for a significant period of time. According to the United Nations (UN), a long-term migrant is "a person who moves to a country other than that of his or her usual residence for a period of at least a year (12 months)" (UNSD, 2017). Yet, not all migrants move for the same reasons, have the same needs or come under the same laws. Hence a terminological distinction is necessary.

This report considers migrants as a large group that includes:

- Those who have emigrated to an EU country from another EU country ('EU migrants'),
- Those who have come to an EU country from a non-EU country ('non-EU born or third-country national'),
- Native-born children of immigrants (often referred to as the 'second generation'), and
- Persons who have fled their country of origin and are seeking international protection.

For the latter, some distinctions are needed. While asylum seekers and refugees are often counted as a subset of migrants and included in official estimates of migrant stocks and flows, this is not correct according to the UN's definition that indicates that "migrant" does not refer to refugees, displaced, or others forced or compelled to leave their homes.

"The term 'migrant' in Article 1.1 (a) should be understood as covering all cases where the decision to migrate is taken freely by the individual concerned, for reasons of 'personal convenience' and without the intervention of an external compelling factor" (IOM Constitution Article 1.1 (a)).

According to recent OECD work the term "migrant" is a generic term for anyone moving to another country with the intention of staying for a certain period of time – not, in other words, tourists or business visitors. It includes both permanent and temporary migrants with a valid residence permit or visa, asylum seekers, and undocumented migrants who do not belong to any of the three groups (OECD, 2016b).

Thus, in this report the following terms are used:

- "Status holder" or "refugee" who have successfully applied for asylum and have been granted some sort of protection in their host country, including those who are recognised on the basis of the 1951 Geneva Convention Relating to the Status of Refugees, but also those benefiting from national asylum laws or EU legislation (Directive 2011/95/EU), such as the subsidiary protection status. This corresponds to the category 'humanitarian migrants' meaning recipients of protection – be it refugee status, subsidiarity or temporary protection – as used in recent OECD work (OECD, 2016b).

- 'Asylum seeker' for those who have submitted a claim for international protection but are awaiting the final decision are referred.
- 'Rejected asylum seeker' for those who have been denied protection status.
- 'Undocumented or irregular migrants' for those who do not have a legal permission to stay.

This report systematically distinguishes which group is targeted by policies and services put in place by the city. Where statistics provided by the cities included refugees in the migrant stocks and flows, it will be indicated accordingly.

The following groups are at the centre of the present study, based on the local data provided:

- *Native-born children of migrant parents or persons with migration background* are Austrian citizens who have at least one parent that was born abroad or holds foreign nationality. These individuals enjoy all political and social rights that come with citizenship. *Vulnerable migrants*: asylum seekers, refugees, unaccompanied minors, migrant women with children and irregular migrants. Within this group, asylum seekers have limited access to labour, higher levels of education, social services and political participation. Where possible, text distinguishes between the different groups according to the definition above.
- *Third-country nationals:* migrants from outside the EU and their families. Individuals in this group benefit from a legal status and access to the labour market, social rights dependent on residence status. They do not benefit from the right to vote.
- Migrants from EU/EEA-member countries (intra-EU mobility) enjoy freedom of movement within EU countries and full access to the labour market. They have right to political participation at the district level.

Statistics of the city of Vienna

The city of Vienna is composed of **23 districts**.

The staff of the city of Vienna: 65 000 persons

Austria **subnational government expenditure** is 34% of public expenditure – OECD34 average = 40.2%.

Vienna population: 1 840 226 inhabitants (as of 1 January 2016)

50% of the population has a **migration background**: They, or at least one of their parents, were born abroad or have foreign nationalities.

35% of the population is **foreign-born**.

27% of the population has **foreign nationality** (share in the total population: 12% EU/EFTA countries and 15% third countries).

27% of the foreign population of voting age are not allowed to vote at the municipal and federal level.

61% of migrants to Vienna have lived in the city for more than ten years.

Most common **countries of origin** of foreign-born Viennese (for more detail, see Table 1.1):

	Share of total population	Share of population with a foreign background
Serbia	5.4%	14.1%
Turkey	4.1%	10.1%
Germany	3.0%	7.9%

In 2015, the city of Vienna received **20 500 asylum applications** (83 500 refugees and asylum seekers who received basic welfare support in all Austria in 2016, during the same time 480 000 asylum seekers transited Austria to reach Germany) and 1 035 unaccompanied minors. In contrast, in 2011 there were 5 195 asylum seekers who received basic welfare support.

Educational attainment of population aged 15+ (Eurostat, 2016)

	Primary	Secondary	Tertiary
Non-migrant	15%	48%	37%
Migrant	29%	41%	30%

Over-qualification: 56% of persons with higher or medium education and qualifications from third countries are employed as unskilled or semi-skilled workers.

Unemployment rate: Without migration background and finished vocational training in Austria oscillated between 4% and 6%, for those born abroad and trained in Austria was between 8% and 18% in 2010-13.

Full-time employment: Educated in Austria: 78% without migration background, 75% with migration background from an EU/EEA country, and 67% with a migration background from a third country. Educated abroad: 75% for EU/EEA – country migrants and 56% for those from a third country.

Share of **self-employment** (including family co-workers): Non-migrants 14%, migrants 9% (Statistics Austria, 2016).

Main sectors where migrants work: Trade (14%), health and social services (12%), hotels and catering (11%), building industry (10%), building maintenance and other services (9%) (Statistics Austria, 2016).

Introduction

This report starts out from the basic observation that local authorities are at the forefront of providing essential services for all migrants, developing a favourable environment for integration, and creating labour and education paths for inclusive societies as well as managing the recent influx of asylum seekers and refugees. This case study aims to identify practices put in place to manage the short- and long-term effects of previous and current migration flows in Vienna, taking into account the relations of local authorities with other public and private stakeholders. The interests of the OECD concern the major challenges posed by migrant integration and the responses undertaken at the local level.

The present report is based on

- An extensive questionnaire designed by the OECD and filled in by representatives of the city of Vienna.
- Expert interviews with: 1) municipal services; and 2) representatives of other public and private institutions and non-governmental organisations engaged in the field of migrant integration with most of them having been named by the representatives of the city of Vienna. The interviews were all conducted during a site visit of the OECD team on 18-19 January 2017 (see the list of participants in Annex A).
- A literature review.
- A document analysis of material provided by the interviewed experts.
- Recently updated data from the Integration and Diversity Monitoring 2017.

The following analysis does not and cannot claim to give a complete picture of all measures regarding migrant and refugee integration implemented by the multitude of public, semi-public and private stakeholders on local, national and international levels active to a varying extent in the city of Vienna. It focuses on the tasks performed by the public local administration in relation to their most important partners, as elaborated on in the OECD questionnaire and in the expert interviews.

Part I. Background and governance of migrant integration

Chapter 1. Migration insights: Flows, stocks and nationalities

Vienna is Austria's metropolis and the capital of Austria. It is the country's economic, cultural and political centre and attracts people from inside and outside the country. The city is home to 182 different nationalities (MA23, 2017) and 50% of the population in Vienna has a *migration background*, meaning the person or at least one of his/her parents was born abroad or has a foreign nationality. The OECD questionnaire results further indicate that the population share of foreign nationals has been steadily increasing (in 1991: 13%, in 2002: 16%, in 2016: 27%). In comparison, the national share of the foreign-born population is distinctively lower, with 15% of its population being foreign-born (OECD, 2017, p. 170). In 2016, in the 20-40 year-old age group, 48% had a migration background and more than half of the children were born to mothers who were born outside Austria (in 2002: 45%, in 2014: 54%).

The most significant migrant origin countries and regions reflect the milestones of immigration history since the end of World War II. At the beginning of the 1960s, Austria faced a growing need for additional labour and started to recruit workers in Turkey (1964) and the Former Yugoslavia (1966). Until today, they form important migrant groups, making up almost one-third of the population with a migrant background. Since the fall of the Iron Curtain and increased movement of people within the European Union, Vienna's and Austria's population composition has been largely impacted by the accession of 12 mostly Eastern European (neighbouring) countries between 2004 and 2007. While population development in Vienna had been stagnating or even shrinking during the 1970s and 1980s, Vienna today is fast growing and is the sixth largest city in the European Union. Its fast population growth is in particular related to immigration from abroad. Since the turn of the millennium, total international net migration has always been positive. In 2016, the net migration was +22 277 persons (MA23, 2017). From 2002 to 2015, the city has grown by 244 600 persons due to international migration, with 130 200 immigrants born in other EU member states and 136 500 born in a third country. In the same time period, international net migration of persons born in Austria was negative (-22 100 persons) (see Figure 1.1). Between 2007 and 2016, the most migrants came from Germany (approx. 19 000), Romania (approx.19 000) and Syria (approx. 18 000) (MA23, 2017).

The high number of Syrians can be ascribed to the large influx of refugees. Like in many big cities in Europe, migration to Vienna peaked in 2015, when refugees mostly all from Syria, Iraq and Afghanistan arrived. From January 2016 to January 2017, the foreign population in Austria increased by 75 000 persons and amounted to 1.3 million persons in total (OECD, 2017, p. 170).

A look into the future (according to prognoses of the Municipal Department 23 and of Statistics Austria) suggests that the city will cross the 2-million-inhabitants threshold before 2030.

Figure 1.1. Net migration in Vienna by broad regions of birth, 2002–15

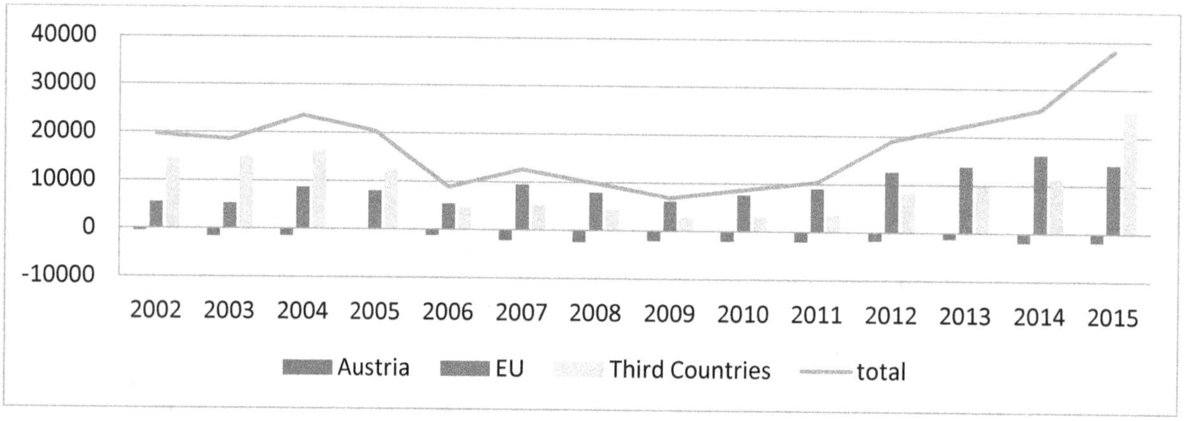

Source: Author, based on Statistics Austria.

As already indicated, intra-EU mobility is key to the city's current population development. More than 40% of the migrant population (285 507 persons) come from EU/EFTA countries. Germany is the most important single sending country followed by eastern European countries such as Poland, Romania, Hungary (see Table 1.1). These figures are in line with overall national trends. Findings in the *OECD Migration Outlook 2017* for Austria show that people originating from Germany (181 700 persons), Serbia (181 700 persons) and Turkey (116 900) constitute the highest number of immigrants to the country in 2016.

Table 1.1. Vienna's foreign-born population by background and gender, 2016

	Background	% of total population	% of foreign born	Women	%
Total population	1 840 226	100.0		947 141	51.5
Austria-born	1 135 324	61.7		588 845	51.9
Foreign-born	704 902	38.3	100.0	358 296	50.8
EU/EFTA	285 507	15.5	40.5	152 393	53.4
Germany	55 361	3.0	7.9	28 641	51.7
Poland	51 639	2.8	7.3	26 656	51.6
Romania	33 224	1.8	4.7	18 286	55.0
Croatia	26 125	1.4	3.7	12 997	49.7
Hungary	25 100	1.4	3.6	13 702	54.6
Other EU, EFTA, assoc. countries	94 058	5.1	13.3	52 111	55.4
Third Countries	419 395	22.8	59.5	205 903	49.1
Serbia	99 082	5.4	14.1	51 682	52.2
Turkey	76 363	4.1	10.8	36 135	47.3
Bosnia and Herzegovina	40 387	2.2	5.7	21 112	52.3
Rest of Europe	51 066	2.8	7.2	27 476	53.8
Africa	27 657	1.5	3.9	10 975	39.7
Asia	101 512	5.5	14.4	46 484	45.8
America	14 666	0.8	2.1	8 099	55.2
Australia and Oceania	1 008	0.1	0.1	511	50.7
Stateless/Convention refugee	7 654	0.4	1.1	3 429	44.8

Note: Background refers to place of birth and citizenship – persons with a foreign background were either born abroad and/or hold foreign citizenship.
Source: Author's calculations, based on MA 23, Economic Affairs, Labour and Statistics.

With regard to gender, EU/EFTA born-migrants from eastern European countries, are more often female (Romania: 55%; Hungary: 54.6%), which might be a result of the pronounced demand for care workers in Viennese households. Among migrants from Africa and Asia, males are currently dominating (share of females from Africa: 39.7%, from Asia: 45.8%; see Table 1.1). Many of them are refugees. However overall, there is no large gender difference between migrants and non-migrants, but only in some specific countries/groups of origin.

Figure 1.2 shows that people with a migration background are more often of working age (here: between 25-65 years of age) than Austrian-born nationals. Among the group from third countries, 67.2% are between 25 and 64 years old. For EU/EFTA-countries, the respective share is only a little lower (64.3%), while this is only the case for half of the population without a migrant background. More than one-fifth of the national-born population has reached retirement age, with the respective shares for foreign-born and non-citizens being much smaller (third countries: 8.1%; EU/EFTA: 13.4%).

Figure 1.2. Age structure of Viennese population by background, 2016

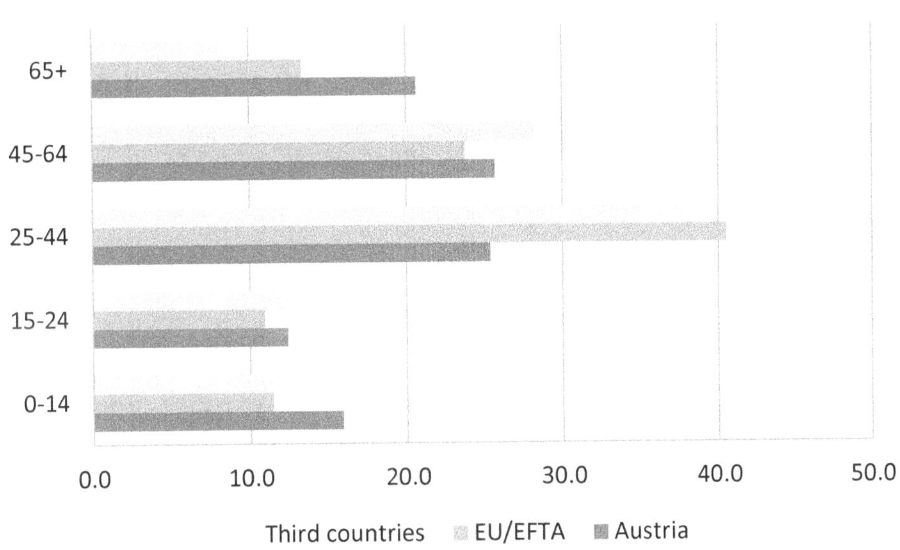

Note: Background refers to place of birth and citizenship – persons with a foreign background were either born abroad and/or hold foreign citizenship.
Source: Author's calculations, based on MA 23, Economic Affairs, Labour and Statistics.

Figure 1.3 presents the length of stay of different groups.[1] It shows the pronounced dynamics of intra-EU mobility: more than one-third of EU citizens came less than five years ago, while the majority of third-country nationals have been in Vienna for a longer period of time, e. g. almost half of them have resided in the city for 10-19 years.

Figure 1.3. Vienna's population by length of stay and background, 2016

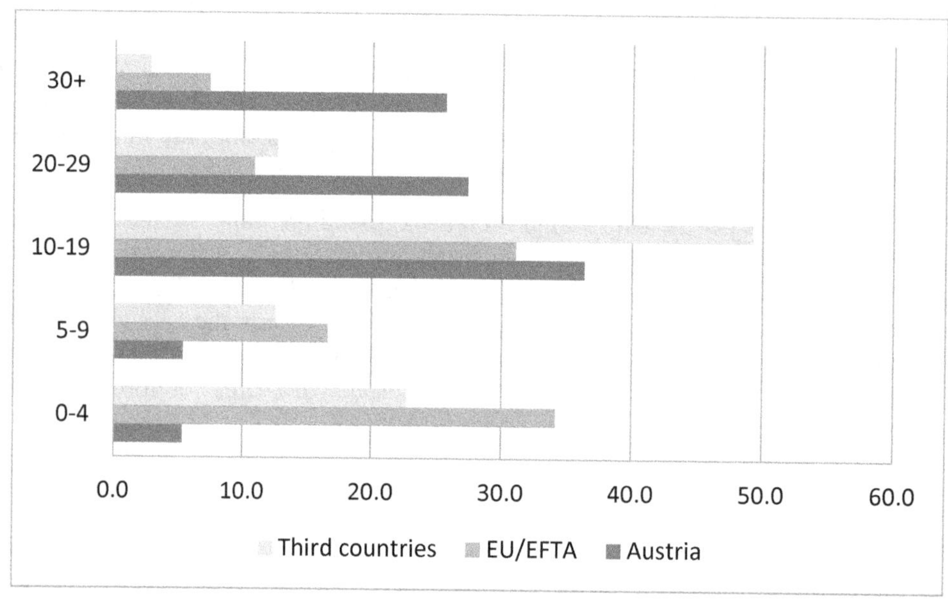

Note: Background refers to place of birth and citizenship – persons with a foreign background were either born abroad and/or hold foreign citizenship. Data on length of stay is only available since 2002.
Source: Author's calculations, based on MA 23, Economic Affairs, Labour and Statistics.

Integration frameworks and regulations for migrants

Austria has seen a major shift in migration and integration policies, which has generated a rather dynamic institutional landscape during the past years. After a long time of considering the issue of migrant integration as marginal at the federal level, this policy area was institutionalised only in 2010 with the enactment of the National Action Plan for Integration (NAP.I). The Action Plan is the result of a collaboration process including relevant ministries, all federal provinces, the Associations of Towns and Cities, Social Partners, non-governmental organisations (NGOs) and experts from the scientific community. NAP.I aims at structuring integration efforts of all parties involved. For further analysis of national institutional background consult OECD work "The labour market integration of immigrants and their children in Austria" (Krause, 2013[1]). However, migrant integration efforts have started earlier on the local level than on the federal level and this sometimes results in divergent targets and measures between the two levels. In previous decades, municipalities and later provinces across the country have institutionalised the agenda of immigrant integration into their strategic plans and established advisory committees at the local level – e.g. Vienna founded the Vienna Integration Fund in 1992 and installed a City Councillor for Integration in 1996 (for further information on the evolution of the integration concept in Vienna, see Annex B).

Since migrants are a highly diverse group (see Table 1.1), regulations hold differences regarding their legal status and their access to the country – and city – of destination and its subsystems. This diversity poses challenges in terms of their integration needs and the policies and measures directed towards them.

For persons from outside the EU/EEA, there is a wide variety of residence permits that have to be obtained before actually entering Austria. Third-country nationals who want to stay for more than six months need a residence permit. These permits are always granted for a specific purpose (work, family reunification) and a specific timeframe as well as in accordance with specific quotas set out each year. (migration.gv.at, n.d.). Fewer than 7 in 1 000 foreign nationals were naturalised in 2013 (2 423 persons), a number that has been quite stable during recent years (2015: 2 967; 2016: 3 055 persons according to MA 23, 2017). These low numbers are the results of a rather strict naturalisation law with the proof of a stable, sufficient and regular income and decent housing conditions for five years prior to naturalisations, representing *inter alia* necessary preconditions. According to the Vienna Integration Monitor, this makes naturalisation a highly selective process in socio-economic terms. Some 18% of third-country nationals were excluded from naturalisation because of these income requirements.

Notes

1. It is important to note, that the figures include all age groups and the whole population, which means that for persons who never migrated, length of stay equals age.

Chapter 2. Vienna's well-being and inclusion[1]

Well-being in Austria is close to the OECD average in many dimensions. However, the average Austrian household has higher adjusted disposal income and face lower labour market insecurity. Compared to the national average, Vienna performs slightly worse in all dimensions of well-being indicators, except for education and accessibility to services (OECD, 2016).

Figure 2.1. Vienna's performance on well-being indicators

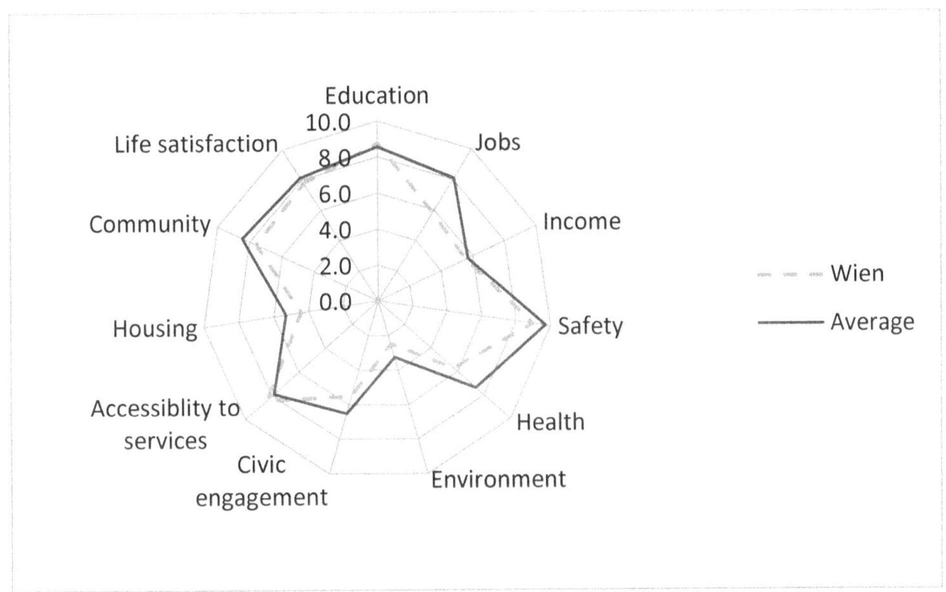

Source: OECD (2016a), Well-being dataset.

Vienna has a high level of economic development and high labour productivity of its working population. In 2014, Vienna's gross regional product amounted to about EUR 84 billion, which is about a quarter of Austria's value added. With 1.84 million inhabitants (2016), about one-fifth of the Austrian population lives in Vienna (20.8%). They generate about a quarter of Austria's gross domestic product (25.6% in 2014). According to AMS (Arbeitsmarktservice Österreich, Public Employment Service) data, foreign nationals represented 24% of the working population in Vienna in 2015. This doesn't include naturalised migrants and native-born children of migrants.

Like many other larger cities, Vienna has evolved into a modern service and knowledge society within the last decades. With a share of 85.3% in gross value added (2014), the services sector is the most important business sector. Nearly one in every five persons in Vienna is active in this sector. However, with 14.7% in gross value added (2014), industry and commerce also account for a significant share, while the primary sector plays a negligible role (0.05%) (MA 23, 2016). The areas of strength of Vienna businesses lie in the fields of life sciences, urban technologies, creative industries and information and communication technology (ICT). In 2015, the location set a record for international settlements with 175 new businesses. Vienna also offers dynamic conditions for start-ups — more than 8 000 companies are founded each year. Yet, typical for a capital region, it also experiences a lot of business deaths and survival is more difficult in the capital than in other regions of the country (OECD, 2017c).

In terms of mobile people, Vienna does not only attract migrants, but also tourists. According to accommodation statistics (MA 23, 2016), the number of overnight stays of tourists (including e. g. congress participants and persons coming for leisure activities) grew by 64.4% from 8.7 million in 2005 to 14.3 million in 2015. More than 40% of the guests came from Germany, the United States, Italy and the United Kingdom. Tourism is thus an important factor in terms of the labour market and productivity.

Vienna is a metropolis of science and research with a long tradition in this respect. The University of Vienna is one of Europe's oldest (founded in 1365) and the largest in the German-speaking countries. As Austria's centre of knowledge, Vienna currently has 195 300 university students (winter semester 2015/16), who make up for more than 10% of the population. In addition, Vienna is also the location of choice for international organisations such as one of the four headquarters of the United Nations, the Organization of the Petroleum Exporting Countries, the International Atomic Energy Agency and the Organization for Security and Co-operation.

Previous OECD research on Austria's migrant population in the education system points to a weaker average educational performance of immigrant students, when compared to native peers (OECD, 2009). This performance gap is largely due to the fact that immigrant students are continuously over-represented in socio-economic less advantaged groups. These findings are in line with findings in Austria when looking at the group of migrants born abroad but who immigrated before they turned 15 years old. For instance while 52% of natives obtained a higher educational degree, only 38% of the group of foreign-born individuals obtained such a degree (Stadt Wien, 2014).

Some 19% of the Viennese population (339 000 persons) were considered as being "at risk of poverty"[2] in 2015 (Europa 2020 indicator). However, the trend over the last years shows a downward tendency; in the year 2008, the rate was 23% (378 000).[3] As it is common for urban centres, the rate is higher than the national average (14% in 2015; 12% in 2008 (City of Vienna, 2012) and clearly under the EU average (25%). Those considered at the highest risk of poverty live in areas with buildings from the 19th century "Gründerzeit", with basic quality housing, and in newer building areas from the building period up to 1960. The lowest at-risk-of-poverty rate can be found in the city centre, in areas with buildings of the 19th century "Gründerzeit" with high-quality housing and in areas with single-family houses and allotments. Migrants belonging to the first generation are at a much higher risk of being poor than non-migrants: their risk-of-poverty rate is more than twice as high. The reasons lie in low incomes due to a lower socio-economic status linked to de-qualification and non-recognition of qualifications. The issue of low socio-economic status can also be observed in children of migrants. According to the outcomes of the Vienna Integration Monitor 2013, migrants from EU new accession countries receive the same low household incomes as third-country-national migrants.

According to the information in the OECD questionnaire provided by MA 18 (Municipal Department 18), the migrant population is distributed unevenly across the city, yet a general dispersion with different concentrations persists (see Figure 2.2). Contrary to many Western European cities, migrants in Vienna are not concentrated along the urban fringe, but rather in the areas adjacent to the city centre in working-class districts that also served as housing areas for migrants when these districts were built up more than 100 years ago.

Figure 2.2. Share of persons born abroad in Vienna, 2016

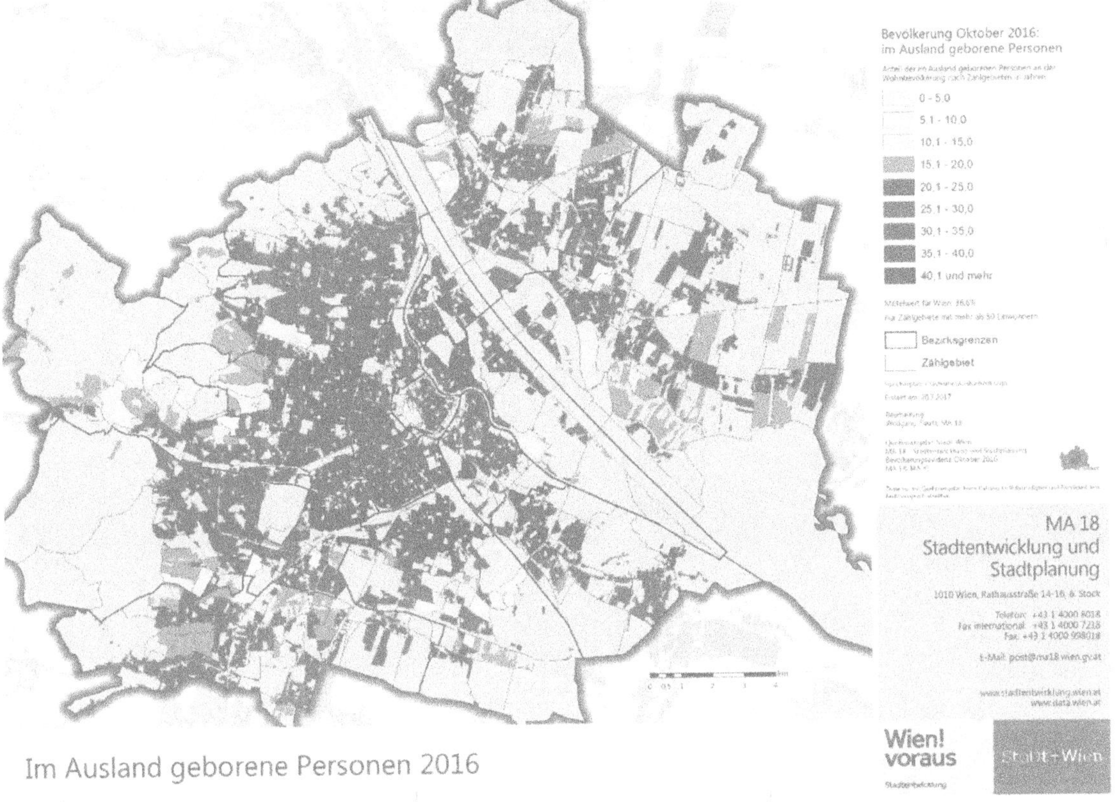

According to a major study on quality of life in Vienna (Verwiebe et al., 2014), there is a concentration of poverty in certain areas of the city. Wage tax statistics (Statistics Austria, 2014) prove disparities in earnings across districts, with e.g. the highest average gross earnings of full-time employed employees in the city centre (EUR 87 921) and the 15th district "Rudolfsheim-Fünfhaus" with the lowest average incomes (EUR 39 064).

Social housing in Vienna was not accessible for third-country citizens until 2006, when an EU Directive regarding the equal treatment of foreigners with a permanent residence status was implemented. Until then, migrants had to rely on the private rental part of the housing market which is concentrated in the working class areas, most of all along the "Belt" (Gürtel), a broad road along the former city walls (in Figure 2.2, the areas in dark blue). With the opening of social housing, further segregation could be impeded, as this segment of the housing market is large and spread all over the city. In the better-off western outskirts of the city, which are characterised by single-family homes, the share of migrants in general is lower, just like in the districts east of the river Danube, which have been mainly developed since World War II.

Notes

1. If not indicated otherwise, this chapter is based on information provided by the representatives of the city of Vienna in their responses to the OECD questionnaire.

2. This level indicates the level below which an individual doesn't earn enough to ensure subsistence (City of Vienna, 2012).

3. OECD questionnaire, 2017.

Part II. Objectives for effectively integrating migrants and refugees at the local level

Chapter 3. Objectives for effectively integrating migrants and refugees at the local level

This part is structured following the *Checklist for Public Action to Migrant Integration at the Local Level*, as included in the Synthesis Report (OECD, 2018), which comprises a list of 12 key evidence-based objectives that can be used by policy makers and practitioners in the development and implementation of migrant integration programmes, at local, regional, national and international levels. This checklist highlights for the first time common messages and cross-cutting lessons learnt around policy frameworks, institutions, and mechanisms that feature in policies for migrant and refugee integration.

This innovative tool has been developed by the OECD as part of the larger study on "Working Together for Local Integration of Migrants and Refugees" supported by the European Commission, Directorate General for Regional and Urban Policies. The checklist is articulated according to 4 blocks and 12 objectives. This part gives a description of the actions implemented in Vienna following this framework.

Checklist for Public Action to Migrant Integration at the Local Level applied to Vienna

Block 1. Multi-level governance: Institutional and financial settings

Objective 1. Enhance the effectiveness of migrant integration policy through improved vertical co-ordination and implementation at the relevant scale.

Objective 2. Seek policy coherence in addressing the multi-dimensional needs of, and opportunities for, migrants at the local level.

Objective 3. Ensure access to, and effective use of, financial resources that are adapted to local responsibilities for migrant integration.

Block 2. Time and space: Keys for migrants and host communities to live together

Objective 4. Design integration policies that take time into account throughout migrants' lifetimes and evolution of residency status.

Objective 5. Create spaces where the interaction brings migrant and native-born communities closer

Block 3. Local capacity for policy formulation and implementation

Objective 6. Build capacity and diversity in civil service, with a view to ensuring access to mainstream services for migrants and newcomers

Objective 7. Strengthen co-operation with non-state stakeholders, including through transparent and effective contracts.

Objective 8. Intensify the assessment of integration results for migrants and host communities and their use for evidence-based policies.

Block 4. Sectoral policies related to the integration

Objective 9. Match migrant skills with economic and job opportunities.

Objective 10. Secure access to adequate housing.

Objective 11. Provide social welfare measures that are aligned with migrant inclusion.

Objective 12. Establish education responses to address segregation and provide equitable paths to professional growth.

Chapter 4. Block 1. Multi-level governance: Institutional and financial settings

Objective 1. Enhance effectiveness of migrant integration policy through improved vertical co-ordination and implementation at the relevant scale

In the federal republic of Austria, tasks are in general divided between the federal level, its federal provinces[1] and local governments. The city of Vienna holds a double function within the Austrian constitutional and administrative framework. It is a city with its own statute and at the same time a federal province. The head of the Vienna City Hall, in his capacity as mayor, heads the city government and is, in addition, the utmost representative of the federal province with provincial governments being decisive stakeholders in the field of migrant integration. In particular, they are responsible for pre-primary and primary education, youth policies, urban and regional planning, and housing (OECD questionnaire, 2017).

According to the representatives of the city of Vienna (OECD questionnaire, 2017), mixed responsibilities are typical for many policy areas: 1) in health, responsibility is shared between the federal government, the provincial governments, and local governments; 2) in housing, the provincial and local governments are decisive; 3) in education, responsibilities are split. The local governments share responsibility with the provincial governments with regard to preschool and primary education; the responsibility for secondary education lies with the provincial governments and the federal government; post-secondary and tertiary education is the sole responsibility of the federal government. Responsibilities are not clear-cut in the policy field of education. Existing federal legislation to enhance equity with regard to inclusiveness and decreasing concentration of migrant students in the lowest tracks, are non-binding, which leads to a significant variance of support structure systems across Austria's provinces, cities and schools (OECD, 2009). Vocational training is a shared competence of the provincial governments, the federal government, and the Social Partners (Chamber of Labour, Economic Chamber, Trade Unions). Employment is the sole responsibility of the federal government. In many areas, like the administration of residence legislation, provincial governments implement federal legislation ("Mittelbare Bundesverwaltung").

The city of Vienna holds a double function within the Austrian constitutional and administrative framework. It is a city with its own statute and at the same time a federal province.

The so-called "Social Partnership" plays an important role in the Austrian political landscape on all levels of government. It is based on the principle of reconciliation of interests which resulted in a specific Austrian form of corporatism – a network consisting of the State, employees' associations (Trade Unions, Chamber of Labour), as well as the employers' association (Economic Chamber, Federation of Austrian Industry). The Chamber of Labour Vienna (AK Vienna) is one of nine federal-provincial entities under the umbrella of the Federal Chamber of Labour. Besides conducting basic research, their main tasks are: 1) to participate in and control legislation from the point of view of employees' interests; and 2) to offer services to employees on issues like labour law, social insurance, worker protection etc. All employees, apprentices, persons on maternity/paternity leave and the unemployed are subject to compulsory membership. AK has about 2 400 employees with one-fourth of them being located in Vienna. The Austrian Economic Chambers (WKÖ) is structured in a similar way. They consist of the Austrian Federal Economic Chamber and nine regional chambers in the federal provinces (in Vienna: WKW) and are divided into seven industry sectors (e. g. crafts and trade, industry, commerce). Strategic areas of business include: 1) representation of interests of its 450 000 members; 2) provision of advice and information to its members; 3) provision of training opportunities.

Allocation of competences for specific integration-related matters (excluding refugees and asylum seekers)

The allocation of competencies in migrant integration in Vienna across different levels of government is displayed in Annex C of this study. With regard to the allocation of competencies for asylum seekers and refugees, Chapter 5 provides insights.

The multi-level institutional mapping for migrant integration in Figure 4.1 demonstrates the city of Vienna within the Austrian Multi-Level Governance System. In addition to state actors, it also includes semi-public actors and non-state actors that are involved with migrant integration. Due to the immense complexity of the system, it only contains the actors referred to in this study and does not include individual linkages between institutions. Rather, it aims to function as an illustration of the linkages and systems described in the text to provide overall insight into the general system and the different roles taken by stakeholders.

Generally, migration is regulated at the federal level, with the Federal Ministry of the Interior responsible for immigration legislation (Aliens Law, Law on Settlement and Residence) and asylum (Asylum Law). The regulatory authority on voluntary migration falls under the responsibility of the Federal Ministry of the Interior (BM.I) and the Federal Ministry of Europe, Integration and Foreign Affairs (BMEIA). An Expert Council for Integration was established in 2010 in the BM.I and was later moved to BMEIA to "translate" the NAP.I into practice. However the NAP.I is not articulated in a way that allows for its implementation and monitoring at the local level. A major shift in migration and integration policies took place after 2010: the creation of the State Secretariat on Integration in the BM.I in the year 2011 with executive and advisory responsibilities, which was transferred to BMEIA in 2014 (Krause, 2013[1]) (OECD, 2013[2]) (OECD, 2014[3]).

Today, the Department of Integration at BMEIA has agenda-setting powers. However, since integration policy is a cross-cutting issue, matters also touch upon the jurisdictions of other federal ministries and levels of government. Due to the federalist governance structure of Austria, integration activities are mainly developed and implemented by provincial and local governments with BMEIA holding a co-ordinating, funding and public relations role. Further, the Federal Ministry of Labour and Social Affairs (BMASK) is responsible for the implementation of labour migration legislation, in particular provisions regarding the "Red-White-Red-Card".[2]

Figure 4.1. Multi-level institutional mapping for migrant integration

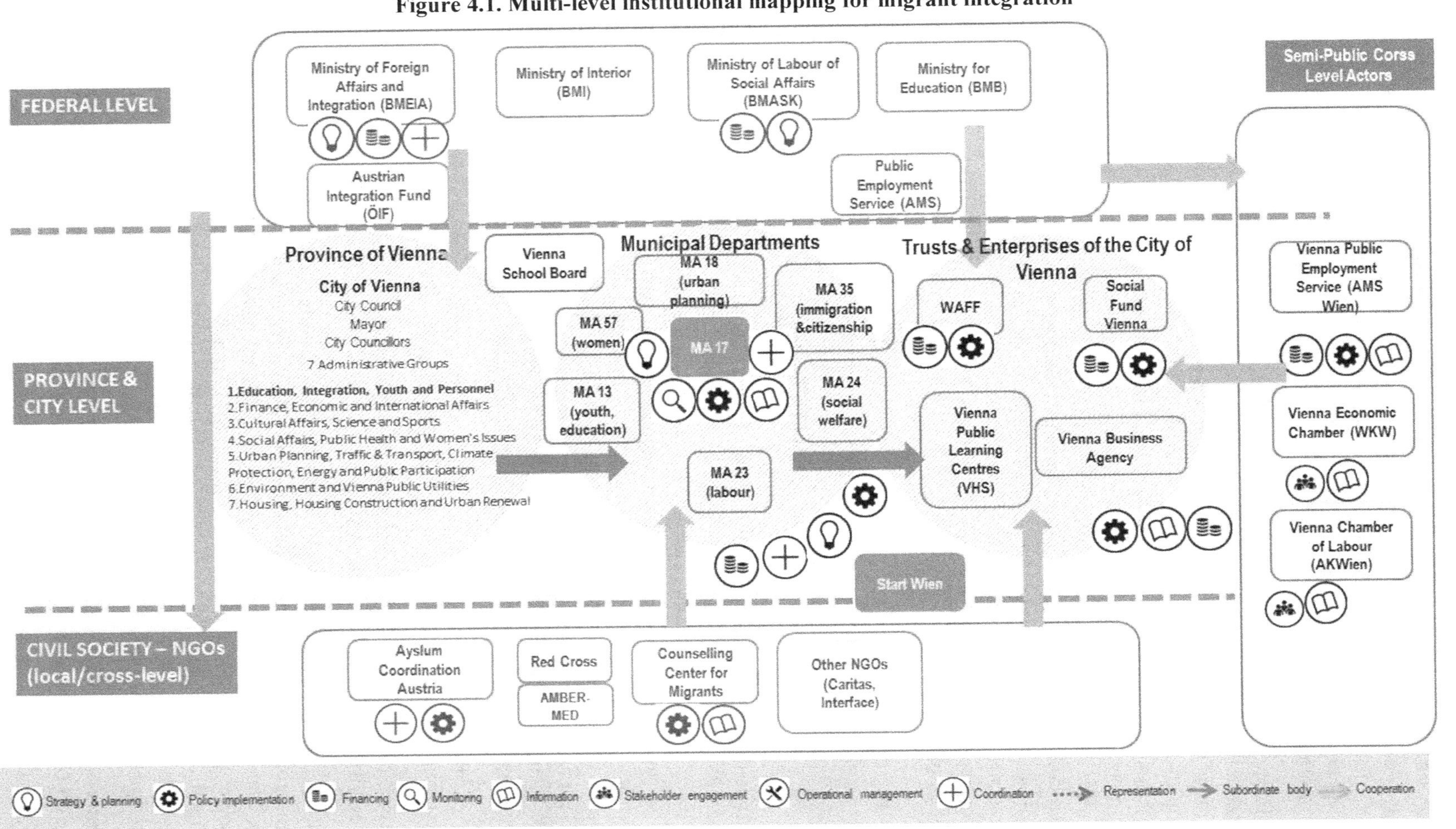

Furthermore, BMEIA is the most important funder of German language courses (via the Public Employment Service, AMS). Only in the province of Vienna, in 2014, more money was spent through the Federal Ministry of Labour, Social Affairs and Consumer Protection (BMASK)/AMS for language training than the total language courses funded by the Federal Office for Immigration and Asylum BMEIA/Austrian Integration Trust (ÖIF) for all of Austria.

The Public Employment Service (AMS) implements labour market policies decided by the federal government. The AMS is structured into 1 federal, 9 regional (federal-provincial) and 104 local organisations. Representatives of employers' and labour organisations (Economic Chamber, Chamber of Labour, the Austrian Trade Union Federation and the Federation of Austrian Industry) are involved at all levels and are instrumental in designing labour market policies (employment programmes of the federal provinces) and in monitoring the AMS' corporate governance. AMS provides measures for everyone in search of labour including migrants, recognised refugees and specific groups as to age or gender, professional groups or (potential) entrepreneurs. In each federal province, AMS has its own budget and develops its own strategy based on labour market specificities in the given entity. In 2015, AMS Vienna had almost 1 100 employees.

Box 4.1. Examples of BMEIA funding for integration

Almost entirely funded by the BMEIA, the "Austrian Funds for Integration" administer the funding of language training and exams included in the "Integration Agreement". Further, it publishes information material on migration and integration. The Integration Agreement is part of the Residence and Settlement Act of the national government (implemented in 2003, revised in 2008 and 2011), which obliges migrants from third countries to acquire B1 level German language skills within two years in order to access the status of long-term resident (ICMPD, 2016: 13). In order to accomplish this goal, they get financial funding to attend language courses from the federal government.

Migration-related national and local co-ordination mechanisms

Between 2015 and 2017, there have been several efforts to achieve better co-ordination between the provinces, BMEIA, AMS and the city's services for migrant integration.

Ensuring better communication and facilitating the exchange of opinions and recommendations was already the aim of the Advisory Board on Integration founded in 2010, including appointed members from the federal government, the federal provinces, the social partners and the five most important non-governmental organisations (NGOs). Chaired by the Austrian Integration Fund, the Advisory Board meets twice a year and has a legal basis. It acts as a regular co-ordination platform with subnational and non-institutional stakeholders on integration issues.

In terms of co-ordination across government levels, provincial governments are in charge of the co-ordination of integration measures with municipalities.

Interaction with neighbouring communes to reach effective scale in social infrastructure and service delivery to migrants and refugees

The Austrian Association of Cities and Towns (Städtebund) represents 252 members – towns and cities in Austria. Founded in 1915, its principal task is to represent the interests of the local level in revenue sharing with the federal government and the federal provinces. The size of its members in terms of population varies considerably, from more than 1.8 million (Vienna) to about 1 000 inhabitants. Membership is voluntary. The association deals with integration in a committee on integration that is chaired by the mayor of St. Polten. The deputy chair in 2017 is Vienna's City Council. In the committee cities discuss as well as consult on integration matters. An important part is sharing experiences and practices among fellow experts.

Objective 2. Seek policy coherence in addressing multi-dimensional migrant needs of, and opportunities for, migrants' integration at the local level

City vision and approach to integration

Vienna has institutionalised the mainstreaming of integration into policy making and diversity management through its own stand-alone Municipal Department for Integration and Diversity (MA 17). The decision to embed the topic of integration and diversity in the regular city administration represents its centrality and importance for the city and its population. The Department has defined its own local integration concept, highlighting the potentials of a diverse population and defining the creation of equal opportunities and participation for all members of society as their goal. Since 2008, it also monitors capacity building and performance on integration indicators and diversity management. Locally, MA 17 engages in co-operation with other relevant departments as well as external stakeholders regarding integration. It engages in intercultural training, counselling and guidance of staff regarding intercultural competence, and leads the mainstreaming processes of policies through advisory boards or topic platforms. MA 17 also acts as the central contact point for NGOs who are engaged in integration matters.

The Vienna Integration Concept forms the basis for integration measures implemented by the city administration. It is updated and reviewed continuously in co-operation with experts as well as with the migrant communities concerned (MA 17, 2016). The four pillars of the concept are:

- language learning and multilingualism
- education and work
- living together and participation
- objectivity (assessment and information).

A welcoming culture forms the basis of the concept, greeting new inhabitants and supporting them to find their way easily and quickly. For example, it includes a welcome package "Start Wien", including important information on basic services and language vouchers for coaching.

Figure 4.2. The Vienna Integration Concept based on MA 17, 2016

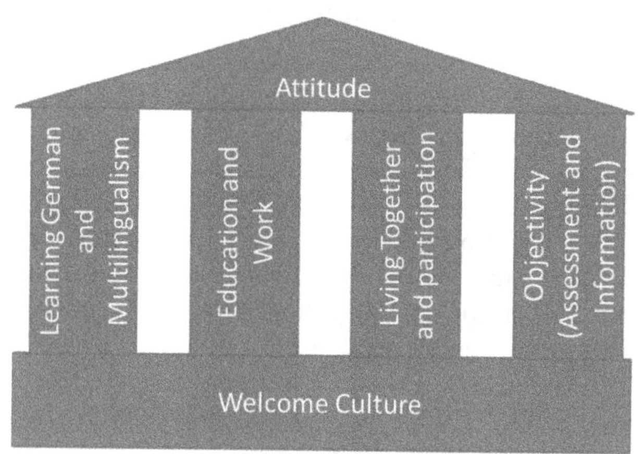

The "roof" of the concept (Figure 4.2) signifies the general human rights approach of the city, highlighting equal opportunities and its clear stance against discrimination, racism and xenophobia. In 2014, the City Council adopted a declaration called "Vienna – City of Human Rights" and since then has focused on creating policies and measures sensitive to human rights and ensuring human rights for all inhabitants, especially vulnerable groups (MA 17, 2016: 9).

Objective 3. Access to, and effective use of, financial resources that are adapted to local responsibilities for migrant integration

Revenues of the total budget of the city of Vienna amounted to EUR 12.5 billion in 2016 and the total spending was EUR 13 billion. The statement of account for MA 17 indicates that in 2016 it spent EUR 9.1 million and had a revenue of EUR 88 511.86.

The main spending of the city of Vienna in 2016 were in the following areas: EUR 2.4 billion in education sports and science, EUR 297 million in arts and culture, EUR 3.1 billion in social welfare and housing support, including the EUR 9.1 million for integration and diversity for MA 17 (Stadt Wien, 2016).

The financial relationship, regarding transfers, tax revenues and sharing of costs between the federal government, provinces and municipalities is regulated by the Austrian finance law (as of 1948). The law foresees that the provinces make use of allocated financial means to fulfil their duties according to shared competencies in the multi-level governance scheme. The federal government acquires 94.8% of all tax revenues in the country, the provinces only 5.2% (BMF, n.d.). The federal government transferred a total of EUR 26 256.9 million in 2015 to its provinces. With 20.96%, Vienna received the highest share of transfers. In addition to this fixed key (as of 2013), calculated based on the size of population, the provinces can claim additional earmarked financial means (Zweckszuweisungen) to cover special requirements (BMI, 2014/2015).

Since 2017, a new law came into force which regulates the balance of contributions across the country, including an infrastructural development scheme for municipalities, which amounts to additional EUR 175 million. Applications for this fund are processed by the federal government. Projects in Vienna receive overall EUR 40 831 million through these means for development such as the construction of new social housing.

Addendum Block 1: Multi-level governance of the reception and integration mechanisms for asylum seekers and refugees

Asylum seekers and refugee regulation

The national agency BFA (Bundesamt für Fremdenwesen und Asyl) subjected to the BM.I is responsible in Austria for processing asylum applications. After asylum applications to the country increased significantly in 2015 (see Chapter 1 of this study), the country witnessed a decline in inflows in 2016 from 88 300 to 42 1000. (OECD, 2017a). From 1 January 2015 to 31 December 2015, the BFA decided on 85 085 applications (BFA, 2015). In 2016, the BFA decided upon 57 439 applications, of which 20 213 (35%) were negative decisions (BFA, 2016). Further in 2016, the agency reported 10 677 persons had to leave the country, 46% of these departures were conducted under compulsion (BFA, 2016).

The agency decides on the following residence titles:

- Persons granted asylum are entitled to reside and enter Austria for a period of three years and have access to services like all other Austrian citizens. After the period of three years has passed and the application is not entitled to review, the person gets unlimited residence.
- Persons granted subsidiary protections receive a temporary residence title with the possibility of extension. Like "asylum", the residence title grants access to all services in the country. According to the BM.I., the residence title can be taken away, once the situation in the country of origin has changed or in exceptional cases, such as if the person has committed a criminal offence.

In June 2016, the Austrian government opted for tightening the country's asylum legislation. A revision of application after three years of residence is now obligatory. Residence status has therefore a somewhat temporary character ("Asyl auf Zeit") (Bundeskanzleramt Osterreich, n.d.). Further, subsidiary protection beneficiaries are entitled to family reunification only after three years of residence. Another significant novelty is that the government is now entitled to declare a state of emergency, which allows for a period of six months a refusal of asylum seekers from transit countries unless proof of immediate danger can be brought forward or the person has relatives in the country (OECD, 2017a).

There is a shared responsibility between the federal government and the provincial governments in the distribution of refugees in the provinces. For this type of shared responsibility, a specific type of legally binding agreement between the federal government and the provincial governments, the "§15 A-Agreements" are used. These agreements, which usually are concluded for periods between one and five years, are reached in negotiations between all nine provincial governments and the federal government and are binding for them (OECD, forthcoming). The general goal is to spread asylum seekers across all federal provinces along the lines of the quota system, based on the size of the population in the province.

Austrian legislation, in line with EU regulations,[3] provides asylum seekers with appropriate accommodation and basic welfare support for as long as the asylum procedure takes and for four more months in the case asylum is granted. Since 2004, there is a renewed nationwide system of refugee support, the so-called basic assistance. Furthermore, the city of Vienna will receive funding from the European Union under the aegis of the Urban Innovative Action Programme ERDF for supplementary infrastructure and strategies for integrating and empowering refugees (OECD questionnaire, 2017). The federal provinces are responsible for organising accommodation and basic welfare support.

Before the inflow in 2015/16, asylum seekers who came to Austria had no access to integration measures like German language courses or vocational training. This turned out to be detrimental for integration, as people tried to access the labour market after the status had been granted, which proved to be difficult due to their long absence from work, language barriers and qualification mismatches. A shift occurred thanks to two changes: the establishment of the *Bundesasylamt* in 2014, which reduced the duration of the assessment of asylum claims and the introduction of local level measures by the city of Vienna, including the "integration from Day 1" concept (see Chapter 4 for more details).

Funding across levels of government

Funding of basic assistance is divided between the federal level and the federal provinces at the ratio of 60:40.Table 4.1 gives an overview of the division of funding across levels of government.

Table 4.1. The cost of integrating refugees by level of government: The case of Austria

Expenditure on refugees, asylum and integration in % of GDP	2014	2015	2016	2017
Federal government	0.14%	0.24%	0.50%	0.50%
Länder + municipalities	0.09%	0.14%	0.23%	0.25%
General state	0.23%	0.37%	0.73%	0.75%

Source: OECD (2017), "Migration Policy Database Nr. 13: Who bears the cost of integrating refugees?", January.

The process step by step: From reception to integration[4]

After a maximum of 48 hours after arrival in Austria, persons who wish to apply for asylum are obliged to submit their application to a local police station in charge of asylum applications (*Schwerpunktdiensstelle*). In this step, registration of name and nationality is processed, the person is questioned for the first time and the data is transferred to the BFA. In a next step, the BFA decides if it is responsible for the application or if the case falls under the Dublin procedure. In the latter case, the person is accommodated in a reception centre (*Erstaufnahmeeinrichtung*) before being transferred to the responsible EU member state. In the former case, the person is temporarily accommodated in a so-called pre-allocation centre (*Verteilerquartier*) before being distributed to a province. In both venues, the pre-allocation centre as well as in reception centres, a first medical check-up takes place. The allocation and the admission to the asylum process are granted by the BFA.

As a reaction to the relatively sudden influx of asylum seekers in 2015/16, the city of Vienna created 8 000 additional places in emergency shelters very quickly. As to the management of temporary emergency accommodation, the city of Vienna (FSW, Head Office for Basic Provisions for Persons Seeking Protection and Asylum) in co-operation with non-governmental organisations (NGOs) has adapted vacant buildings belonging to the city and additionally rented private property to accommodate asylum seekers. The aim is to avoid urban concentration of refugees; therefore the focus is on flat-sharing communities with three or four people in one flat. At the same time, an appeal was made to the population to propose housing for this purpose. At the end of the year 2016, 63% of the 20 500 asylum seekers receiving basic welfare support in Vienna resided in private accommodations and 37% were hosted in 90 organised shelters. Once recognised as refugees, a provision of housing is possible under certain circumstances (via the Counselling Centre for the Homeless "bzwo" run by FSW). Otherwise, they have to rely on the housing market or on private help via the support of specialised NGOs (see the section below). For example, there are partnerships and grants with People's Aid Austria[5] or a deposit fund for the rent of flats (Interface).

Furthermore, measures were initiated regarding healthcare, e.g. immediate health insurance upon registration and visits by doctors on call to the accommodation facilities at regular intervals (OECD questionnaire, 2017). For unaccompanied minor refugees, flat-sharing communities with social educational support were established. Refugees with disabilities or with chronic diseases – an even more vulnerable group – have been provided with specialised housing.

School-age children are obliged to attend lessons during all the steps and right after arrival. Even though asylum seekers are not allowed to work, they can take up charitable tasks for the community in which they are allocated to, after a period of three months of stay.

Once asylum is granted and people have access to the labour market, advisors at the public employment service (AMS) can instantly use the information from the education database to help people find suitable jobs and feed these data into the so-called Competence Check, a measure designed by AMS for recognised refugees. Up to now, about 6 000 recognised refugees have taken part in the Competence Check in all federal provinces, though most of all in Vienna. These courses last for five weeks and are carried out by private educational institutions for the AMS. They check language proficiency, educational level, professional experience, personal interests and motivations. Furthermore, they help with and inform individuals about applying for a job as well as norms and values in Austria.

Key observations: Block 1

- Due to the federalist governance structure of Austria, integration activities are mainly developed and implemented by provincial and local governments with the federal Ministry for Integration and Foreign Affairs holding a co-ordinating, funding and public relations role.
- The city of Vienna is both a city and a federal province; hence it holds a double function and is entrusted with competences in both government levels. This way, the city holds large responsibilities in early education and housing matters that are generally shared between the provincial and the local level. Also, the double function gives the city greater access to decision-making processes as it has the ability to engage with the federal level from two standpoints.
- The National Action Plan for Integration demonstrates a collective endeavour between all levels of government to pool integration efforts across government levels and is an anticipated bridge for sectoral fragmentation of integration-related tasks across ministries, municipal departments and agencies. Further, an Advisory Board on Integration acts as a regular co-ordination platform between members of the government,

the federal provinces, the social partners and the five most important NGOs.

- Vienna has institutionalised the mainstreaming of integration into policy making and diversity management through its own stand-alone Municipal Department for Integration and Diversity (MA 17). The Department develops and implements its own measures and project for migrants, facilitates the mainstreaming of integration and diversity matters into local policy making and conducts diversity and integration monitoring to evaluate progress made in the city.

- The Austrian federal government and the provincial governments share responsibility in the distribution of asylum seekers in provinces. A legally binding agreement is used to structures this co-operation. Asylum seekers are spread across all federal provinces along the lines of a quota system based on the size of the population in the province. Funding for basic assistance for asylum seekers is divided between the federal level and the federal provinces at the ratio of 60:40. The federal provinces are responsible for organising accommodation and basic welfare support. In Vienna, 8 000 additional places in shelters were set up in 2015/16. Further, the city decided to extend language courses to asylum seekers and complement federal integration measures that merely targeted people that had already received recognition.

Notes

1. The term of "federal provinces" is used here as a generic term to refer to the constituent regions of a federation. They have specific names depending on the federation: states or provinces in Austria (*Bundesländer*) (OECD, 2017). The Austrian state is composed of nine federal provinces that that have their own legislative bodies, executive organs and financial management. Certain legislative matters are reserved for the provinces (Republic of Austria, n.d.).

2. This card targets qualified personnel from third countries.

3. Directive 2013/33/EU of the European Parliament and of the Council of 26 June 2013 sets out standards for the reception of applicants for international protection.

4. If not otherwise indicated, this section is based on information provided by the Austrian Ministry of Interior (BM.I).

5. See www.volkshilfe-wien.at/wohnungslosenhilfe/wohndrehscheibe/.

Chapter 5. Block 2. Time and space: Keys for migrants and host communities to live together

Objective 4. Design integration policies that take time into account throughout migrants' lifetimes and status evolution

Use integrated approaches from Moment Zero/Day One

The Vienna Social Welfare Fund and the Municipal Department for Integration and Diversity (MA 17) jointly created the operative system of "integration from Day 1" and very close co-operation started on this matter. It aims to help newcomers settle in Vienna as quickly as possible. Important pillars are language learning from the beginning and the access to "Start Wien".[1] Start Wien functions on a one-stop-shop principle and serves different kinds of migrant and refugee groups that want to settle in the city. As soon as new asylum seekers, refugees and migrants register at the Municipal Department 35 (Immigration and Citizenship), they are offered individual counselling by employees of MA 17 in 25 languages. This first consultation clarifies the migrant's concrete information needs. The following "Start Coaching" is split up into several modules (e.g. labour market, education, housing, healthcare, human rights, legislation and society) and after attending an introduction event, asylum seekers, refugees and migrants are given vouchers for language courses (for EU citizens worth EUR 150, for third-country nationals EUR 300, as they are subject to the Integration Agreement). Originally implemented for third-country nationals as of 2008, the need to broaden the measure to include newcomers from the European Union was soon realised, and accomplished in 2011 (Reeger and Enengel, 2016). As of 2015, Start Coaching Vienna is also specifically offered to asylum seekers upon arrival in Vienna. MA 17 and FSW jointly developed "Start Wien Refugees". Many network partners are active in this measure: MA 17 and MA 35, FSW, WAFF, AMS, Social Partners, the Vienna Business Agency, Interface, and the Counselling Centre for Migrants.

From 2016 onwards, the process was intensified together with the Public Employment Service (AMS, which has been a longstanding partner engaging in this field). An important outcome of the co-operation is the competence check (see Chapter 3), including educational coaching and positioning based on skills assessment aiming for integration into the national education system. (AWZ, n.d. Version 3). Further, the education database, which gathers information on individual education and qualification profiles, in German classes for example, includes validation processes of migrants' and refugees' competences. The common goal of MA 17, FSW and AMS Vienna is continuous integration without system discontinuities. Accordingly the city has adapted the aspect of timing into their integration concept realising that the time during asylum procedures can be used for educational assessment and other measures. This goes beyond the approach of the national level (BMEIA), where integration measures are implemented at a later stage for asylum seekers, mostly once asylum has been granted.

Consult with migrant communities and actors with longstanding experience in integration issues

According to the representatives of the city of Vienna (OECD questionnaire, 2017), there are no institutionalised measures for the involvement of migrants in local decision-making processes or as to other aspects of their participation in the city's public and political life. Vienna does not have a permanent co-ordination platform with non-governmental organisations (NGOs) and migrant associations discussing strategic integration questions. The Vienna Integration Conference was abolished in 2009. Despite the lack of institutionalised dialogue, local integration vision and initiatives are developed in consultation with relevant groups as it has been the case for the Start Wien project. As mentioned in Objective 5 below, continuous dialogue is ensured through the meetings that MA 17 holds at the district or city level covering specific topics. Through this practice MA17 communicates and co-operates with more than 400 migrant associations.

As to voting, naturalised migrants have voting rights at all levels of representation (district council, city council); EU citizens can only vote on the district level; and third-country nationals do not have any voting rights at all. In the view of municipal officers, limited voting rights can lead to reduced feelings of integration, which can be widespread in some districts with a high share of migrants.

Objective 5. Create spaces where the interaction brings migrant and native communities closer

Already in 2005/06 the city conducted a large study stressing the importance of creating functional public spaces to foster integration. It highlighted that public spaces could become indicators for accomplishing social integration and influence urban planning (Stadt Wien, 2006).

Encourage bottom up initiatives that fosters integration and participation

On top of city's awareness of the importance of public spaces, several other measures have been put in place to foster proximity between different groups in the city and sustain civic engagement.

One important tool for ensuring proximity at the level of districts and neighbourhoods are the regular meetings with civil society organisations, including migrant organisations held in the local offices of MA 17 (OECD questionnaire, 2017). These meetings focus on specific topics and mainly aim at an exchange of views and ideas. Furthermore, all residents have the right to address petitions to the City Council on any issue. These petitions have to be discussed in the respective working groups of the City Council.

The project Migra-Bil, co-ordinated by MA 17, provides representatives of associations as well as individuals with a migrant background with the opportunity to acquire basic knowledge in the areas of voluntary work, event organisation and intercultural communication. Participation is free of charge (Stadt Wien, n.d.).

The Vienna Charter was a unique initiative in Europe (OECD questionnaire, 2017). It provides the framework for good neighbourly relations by actively promoting dialogue between citizens and building solidarity. It is a written agreement between people who live in Vienna, an agreement they have reached mutually and out of their own conviction. The city of Vienna merely facilitated the process in which people could express their views on how good neighbourly relations should function and what they would do to contribute to them. It was not about what politicians or the city administration should do, but rather about what each individual could do to improve the way people live together in their city. The Viennese themselves chose the topics for the charter and actively participated in its development. They were able to participate both on and off line. Based on the input provided, an advisory committee identified what the charter should address (OECD, n.d.).

In total, 651 charter talks were held in all districts of Vienna in 2012 and at nearly every kind of venue imaginable (in pubs, offices, schools, private flats, parks, and public swimming pools). Some 8 500 people participated, investing a total of 12 700 hours into discussing good neighbourly living. The participants represented a true cross-section of Vienna's population: children, young people, senior citizens, blue and white-collar workers, entrepreneurs, persons not in employment as well as people with different mother tongues and countries of origin, people with special needs, people with different religious beliefs, world views and political opinions, and people with different sexual orientations.

Although there had been doubts during the planning phase and at the beginning of the process as to whether it would even be possible to create a single text from the many, possibly diverging opinions, the results were very surprising. The vast majority of the contributions and wishes overlapped strongly in several key issues, so that the main contents and core elements of the text were very clear. They were assembled into the "Vienna Charter", which was presented to the public as the result of the process in a press conference in November 2012.

Communication with citizens on integration issues takes place at neighbourhood level

Communication with the native population about immigration is also part of the city's approach to integration. Three lines of measures are currently applied (OECD questionnaire, 2017):

- **Neighbourhood offices – intercultural work on site**: The teams of the three field offices of MA 17 provide services on site for all Viennese. They promote good neighbourly relations in the districts and in the city. They are contact points for all questions, ideas and suggestions regarding good relations in the neighbourhood and how to improve them.
- **Information talks in the districts**: In light of the increased number of migrants and the recent influx of refugees into the country, many people have concerns about how this will affect their lives in the city. The city tries to address fear and questions by giving information talks about migration and integration in district offices of the MA 17. The teams of the local offices of MA 17 are available to discuss all questions regarding this topic with the people in the districts.
- **Voluntary conflict workers**: This measure aims to promote conflict management in case of neighbour disputes that can sometimes be linked to cultural awareness issues and poor communication. It has been operated for many years. Skilled conflict workers support neighbours in finding solutions to their conflicts. Voluntary conflict workers are a free service in addition to the mediation services of the neighbourhood service "Wohnpartner" for municipal social housing. The service is also available for people who live in private housing.

During the peak in inflows of refugees, the city of Vienna tried to reassure its citizens by quickly housing asylum seekers in federal reception centres, and organised public events in these sites. MA 17 supported the messaging around managing asylum seekers inflows around a positive approach to preventing a feeling of insecurity.

Another initiative worth mentioning in this context is Asylum Coordination Austria (Asylkoordination Österreich), a large platform of NGOs dealing with migrants and asylum seekers and their situation in Austria. Established in 1991, its main tasks and goals are to inform and sensitise the public to the problems and needs of migrants and refugees, organising workshops, discussion and to publish on these matters (see www.asyl.at). Furthermore, meetings with partner NGOs aim at an exchange of experience, organising seminars and training courses. They also seek to give advice to policy makers and are embedded in European networks.

Key observations: Block 2

- Vienna places considerable importance on starting integration from Day 1, meaning the day of arrival. The city's one-stop-shop support structure "Start Wien", which includes language courses and targeted counselling, is a good example facilitating an early integration process that is adapted to the needs of different migrant groups.
- The city is very active in opening consultative channels and spaces for interaction between native and migrant communities. Neighbourhood offices of MA 17 regularly consult with over 400 civil society and migrant organisations having long-standing integration experiences.
- The city is engaged in offering information to all citizens on policies related to migrant integration, for instance the MA 17 field offices organise information talks in the districts. During the peak of refugee arrivals of asylum seekers the city organised public events in federal reception centres to reassure its citizens.
- Further, the city facilitated the creation of the "Vienna Charter", a document that defines a framework for good neighbourhood relations. This document was developed through a unique participative process open to everyone, and involving 8 500 participants.
- Institutionalised entry points for migrant participation in policy-making processes at the local level are still lacking.
- Despite the city awareness of the importance of public spaces for fostering integration this study didn't collect significant evidence of public spaces attractive for different groups where they can meet and develop common interests (Barcelona could provide some interesting practices), or encouraging bottom-up initiatives for creating spaces that foster integration (Paris could provide some interesting practices in this sense).

Notes

1. Start Wien mainly aims to provide basic information about aspects like education, health, and accommodation, as well as cultural aspects of values and living together.

Chapter 6. Block 3. Local capacity for policy formulation and implementation

Objective 6. Capacity and diversity in civil service, with a view to ensuring access to mainstream services for migrants and newcomers

As previously mentioned, the tasks of the Municipal Department for Integration and Diversity (MA 17) include a provision of information and advice concerning the implementation of diversity management in all parts of administration and monitoring of all municipal departments in the context of the diversity management measures. Since 2008 this includes assessing whether city services, staff policies and organisational structures have been adapted to mirror the ethnic, social and cultural diversity of Vienna. It analyses 43 departments and institutions observing general improvement over time. In its last analysis in 2016 it observed a positive tendency with a rising number of departments offering multi-lingual services as well as the number of departments embedding diversity management at their strategic level. It also observed that shares of employees of foreign origin in management positions and among youth remain fairly low. MA 17 observed that awareness-raising efforts are key to helping other departments understand the role that their work can play in advancing integration goals, and incorporating concrete targets into their plans. MA 17's training offered to other municipal departments, combined with the monitoring exercise on diversity and integration, have been instrumental in convincing other practitioners working on diverse policy portfolios to put integration high in priority on their departments' agendas.

Related to one of the four pillars of the Vienna Integration Concept – "Objectivity (assessment and information)" (see Chapter 3) – MA 17 sees providing information and raising awareness among the public and the administration as one of its focal tasks. The city administration needs detailed information on current developments regarding immigration and integration in order to plan sustainably and implement appropriate actions and strategies in core fields like housing, education, healthcare, infrastructure and public transport.

The city is very active in peer-learning experiences, city partnerships and networks. For instance, as part of the EU project "CENTROPE Capacity", the city of Vienna partners with cities in the Czech Republic, Hungary and the Slovak Republic. The 23 districts of the city have their own municipal partnerships with many different international cities across the world, which serve as platforms to share information and co-operate in various policy areas, in particular in cultural and educational matters (Stadt Wien, n.d.c).

One example in the policy area of migration is the city's engagement in the peer network Mediterranean City-to-City Migration Project (MC2CM) since 2015, as the only non-Mediterranean city jointly with Lisbon, Lyon, Madrid, Beirut, Tangier, Tunis, Turin and Amman (Stadt Wien, 2015c). The network serves as a platform for the exchange of individual experiences, challenges and strategies in the field of local urban migration and integration and aims at finding new and innovative policy solutions and implementing these as pilot projects. The platform was initiated by the International Centre for Migration Policy Development (ICMPD). It is also supported by United Cities and Local Governments (UCLG) and UN Habitat, and is funded by the European Commission and the Swiss Agency for Development and Cooperation (SDC).

Objective 7. Strengthen co-operation with non-state stakeholders, including through transparent and effective contracts

As mentioned in Chapter 3, Social Partnership plays an important role in the political context of Austria as well as Vienna. The city government often relies on non-governmental organisations (NGOs) to address migrant integration issues in their name by delegating tasks. This includes funding, but also collaboration in projects and consultation for the elaboration of integration policies. However, as highlighted in Objective 4 there are no institutionalised platforms for consultation with NGOs, migrant organisation and private sector actors involved in integration issues. Such mechanism could enhance information exchange about integration priorities that actors face day to day on the ground and coordinate operations around specific issues (i.e language course provision, etc.). In this sense Athens and Barcelona have put in place constructive coordination practices with non-state actors.

In addition to the outsourcing of tasks, the city of Vienna and several trusts and funds belonging to the city engage in migrant integration, even though none of the funds is dedicated to migration-related issues only. They target the whole population (FSW) or the whole workforce (WAFF, see below; Vienna Business Agency). NGOs are involved both directly with the city or through its funds, oftentimes targeting certain migrant groups, and getting funding for their projects, but also by being involved in consultation processes. Social Partners and AMS (Public Employment Service, see Chapter 3) focus on labour market issues and co-operate with the city, its funds and NGOs.

Table 6.1 lists examples of the city of Vienna's outsourced projects and tasks.

Table 6.1. Overview of outsourced projects or co-operation with the city of Vienna's involvement

Name	Description/purpose	Finances	Link
Vienna Social Fund (FSW)	Founded in 2001, this fund's terms of operation and finances lie with the city of Vienna. The municipality sets targets but manages the fund according to private-sector principles. A large share of the budget is used for care and support, mostly for the elderly, for handicapped persons and for the homeless. As an immediate reaction to the current inflow of refugees, the head of FSW, Peter Hacker, was appointed as refugee co-ordinator for the city of Vienna in 2015. Under his guidance the fund is in charge of administering the basic welfare support for asylum seekers (up to a projected number of 36 000 persons at the end of 2016). The planned expenditures in the year 2016 amounted to EUR 290 million. FSW's staff comprises about 1 600 employees and they co-operate with more than 150 social service providers and partner organisations at about 800 locations all across Vienna.	In 2016, the FSW's budget was enlarged to EUR 1.74 billion, with EUR 1.09 billion coming from the city of Vienna and EUR 0.65 billion from customers' contributions.	www.fsw.at
Vienna Employment Promotion Fund (WAFF)	WAFF implements national labour market policies at the local level. It works in close co-operation with the Vienna Public Employment Service, the BMASK and the local branches of the Social Partners (Chamber of Labour, Chamber of Commerce). WAFF focuses on job training for persons who	The budget amounted to EUR 46.5 million in 2015.	www.waff.at

Name	Description/purpose	Finances	Link
	are already involved in the labour market but also provides special programmes, e. g. for women or persons at risk of unemployment. Moreover, as part of the Vienna Start Coaching it provides a module on the labour market and job opportunities. Although open to all Viennese, about 47% of their clients are migrants, a share that is above the share in the total workforce. When developing new measures, WAFF makes proposals that have to be approved by the city and the Public Employment Service. WAFF currently employs about 210 persons, one-third of which has a migrant background.		
Interface Vienna	The core task is to provide newly arrived migrants (all age groups) with language courses and education measures as well as counselling for refugees. The interface is a certified language school where migrants can take exams for ÖSD A1 to B2. In the year 2015, more than 10 600 migrants were in touch with Interface Vienna. The organisation is a GmbH (limited liability company) owned by the city of Vienna and has about 130 employees.		www.interface-wien.at
Vienna Business Agency	A fund owned by the city of Vienna and actively promoting the development and strengthening of the business location of Vienna. It provides local as well as international enterprises with free counselling, funding and the provision of subsidised working spaces. One department is specialised in helping migrants set up a business and become entrepreneurs.		www.wirtschaftsagentur.at
Beratungszentrum für MigrantInnen (Counselling Centre for Migrants)	One example is a major NGO active in the field of labour market integration. Founded in 1983, it is one of the oldest and largest counselling institutions for labour migrants in Austria and also serves as one of the five Contact Points for the Recognition and Assessment of Qualifications Obtained Abroad (AST; funded by BMASK, federal-provincial funds and in Vienna also by WAFF).Target groups are migrants living in Vienna (migrants, Austrian citizens with a mother tongue other than German and status holders). They offer help and advice as to entering the labour market and education measures as well as regarding social benefits in a wide range of different languages.	The Counselling Centre for Migrants is funded by BMASK, AMS, WAFF, the European Social Fund (ESF) and MA 17.	www.migrant.at

MA 17 funds a large variety of other NGOs and their projects regarding migrant integration, with the threshold being EUR 5 000. Below that amount of money, they are called "small-scale projects" and beyond "large-scale projects". In terms of content, projects can either be designed to foster intercultural sensibility and competence or focus on concrete measures for a successful integration (e.g. language acquisition, education, legal counselling). In 2016, 26 large-scale projects and a large variety of small-scale projects were funded.

Objective 8. Intensify the assessment of integration results for migrants and host communities and their use for evidence-based policies

Since 2008, the Vienna Integration and Diversity Monitor publishes data about the city's current situation regarding integration and diversity, illustrating socio-economic aspects of local migration that demonstrate gaps between migrant and non- migrant groups with the aim of creating equal opportunities for all population groups. It observes eight subject areas where integration takes place: equality and participation; education; employment and labour market; income and social security; health; housing; infrastructure; public space and living together. The insights provide a good evidence-based proxy for assessing the impact of integration policies implemented and are used as a compass and should guide strategic developments. An important characteristic of this monitoring is that data of other municipal departments are synthesised into the report, allowing for a comprehensive understanding of the city's achievements and challenges. Yet, the extent to which the results influence policy making and lead to possible changes remain unclear.

A second tool of the municipality is a survey with which perceptions of successful migration is investigated. It is called the Zuwanderungs Monitor and is published regularly. The latest version (2017) indicates that there is a tendency to support increased migration and cultural diversity in the city. For example, many Viennese indicate that they agree with the fact that foreign nationals who have been living in the city should have the right to vote in local elections. In addition, it would be interesting to understand to what extent migrants have the same understanding of what integration means and their perception of "successful" integration.

Key observations: Block 3

- Awareness-raising efforts and training are a key measure used by MA 17 to heighten the sensitivity of departments for their role in advancing integration goals, and incorporating concrete targets into their plans. Further, regularly conducted diversity monitoring helps to assess developments diversity management according to defined benchmarks.
- The city government often relies on NGOs to address migrant integration issues and directly delegates tasks to them. This includes funding, but also collaboration in projects and consultation for the elaboration of integration policies. Further, a variety of funds operated by the city engage in migrant integration within their regular efforts to address more general social needs and therewith also build capacity beyond early integration services.
- The city could consider setting up permanent consultation mechanisms with migrant associations and CSOs involved on integration matters. The dialogue could aim at both, ensuring migrant views are taken into account in local decision making and structure coordination among non-state actors operating in this field.
- The city's "Integration and Diversity Monitor" is an important monitoring tool depicting integration developments in eight policy areas. It allows for comparisons to previous years covering a variety of sectors involved in integration.

Chapter 7. Block 4. Sectoral policies related to the integration

Objective 9. Match migrant skills with economic and job opportunities

Successful integration through participation in the labour market is key at the local level. . It facilitates access to housing, and enables independence from social welfare. Also, it often enables better social integration because people can better afford leisure activities, build networks linked to labour and face less discrimination on the basis of unemployment. Consequently the city's Integration and Diversity Monitor (Stadt Wien, 2014) stresses the aim of creating equal chances for employment for migrants and non-migrants and making use of potentials such as multilingualism, that are to the benefit of the whole society.

Recognition of education and training qualifications is a key mechanism for making foreign-born fit for local labour market demands. However, data from the city of Vienna show a clear gap in employment results of third-countries migrants not educated in Austria and those born abroad, but trained in the country of residence. The first group scoring 11 percentage points lower in the employment rate than the second (Stadt Wien, 2017: 88). This systematic gap in accessing the labour market between third country foreign-born hints at discrimination for migrants without an Austrian education or training certificate, as their education does not differ (OECD questionnaire, 2017). For EU/EAA-counties this does not make a difference, 75% of those not educated in Austria are employed compared to 75% of their peers educated in Austria. Further, third-country nationals, whether educated abroad or not, have the lowest employment rate (56% for those not educated in Austria and 67% for those educated in Austria). Further, the data show that the employment rate for women is significantly less than for men. The difference is particularly large for women who were educated abroad and those coming from third countries but were educated in Austria.

One concern is unemployment rates for so-called "NEETs" (young people who are neither in training nor education nor employment). In 2016, 22 000 of the 15-24 year-olds were NEETs, showing an increase of 14% from 2007 to 2016. A particularly large share, 66% of the NEETs educated in Austria is foreign-born or has at least one migrant parent.

Even though decreasing, migrant women who were not educated in Austria make up the highest share of NEETs with 29% in 2016. Also of note is the share of children of migrant parents educated in Austria increased from 17% to roughly 20%, while the shares for other sub-groups decreased (Stadt Wien, 2017, p. 101).

Lower qualification and less-well-paid jobs for migrants and their children are also reflected in the annual income for households. The household income gap between foreign-borns and native-borns increased continuously during the past ten year for people in Vienna. Income for people without a migration background has risen by up to 25% to EUR 24 000 (net, per annum), while it has risen by 4%, so below the inflation rate, to an average of EUR 16 200 (net, per annum) for households from third countries (Stadt Wien, 2017). Households from the new EU states are located in between with EUR 18 400 (net, per annum), while EU-14 households have the highest income of EUR 26 500 (net, per annum) (Stadt Wien, 2017).

The issue of de-qualification became a prominent policy matter with the EU accession rounds of 2004 and 2007. Back then, many migrants with high qualifications started to come to Austria and did not find jobs corresponding with their qualifications at least at the beginning of their stay with the reasons being manifold (language barriers, discrimination, labour market mismatches, barriers to recognition of qualifications). This is still a challenge today. According to the latest integration monitoring, only 10-18% of native-born Austrians or persons with parents from EU/EFTA countries educated in Austria, work in a job below their educational qualification, while this is the case for 56% for third-country nationals educated abroad and 46% educated in Austria as well as 45% of migrants from EU/EFTA states (Stadt Wien, 2018, p. 97).

In Austria, labour market issues are not regulated on the local city level but at the federal level, leaving the city with limited margin of manoeuvre in this issue. Nevertheless, the city of Vienna has established WAFF, which partners with AMS, the Counselling Centre for Migrants and other key stakeholders to engage and contribute to labour market integration.

In Vienna, the Counselling Centre for Migrants serves as one of the four Contact Points for the Recognition and Assessment of Qualifications Obtained Abroad (AST) in Austria. In 2013, this initiative was implemented at the federal level by BMASK in order to tackle the ongoing de-qualification of migrants and help them with the recognition of qualifications obtained abroad. These regional contact points provide multi-lingual guidance and counselling related to the recognition of qualifications free of charge. The issue of recognition of qualifications is very complex with individual cases needing individual solutions. Regulations concerning the recognition of qualifications have been established on many different levels (national, federal provinces, professional associations) with AST Vienna being quite successful in manoeuvring the respective legal provisions and the pronounced utilisation of that offer, proving its importance.

The Vienna 2020 Qualification Plan addresses a major challenge of the Vienna labour market, namely the growing demand for a qualified workforce and the declining chances of people with a low level of qualification (see Box 7.1). According to MA 23, about 23% of the economically active population (220 000 persons in the age group between 25 and 65 years) have compulsory education only. Large parts of the low-qualified people are migrants or have a migration background. The 2017 diversity and integration monitor state that numbers for Viennese only completing compulsory education is 7% higher for people with migration background educated in Austria than for people without a migration background Overall, foreign-born groups educated abroad have lower educational attainment results counting higher percentages of persons without degree and larger low-qualification shares (Stadt Wien, 2017).

Box 7.1. The Vienna 2020 Qualification Plan

The key target group of the Vienna 2020 Qualification Plan are young people who have not had any education beyond compulsory schooling (Grade 9). The measure actively seeks to reduce the share of this group in the total workforce until the year 2020. Multiple stakeholders are engaged in this process: the city of Vienna, AK Vienna, AMS, WAFF, WK Vienna, BMASK, the Vienna group of the Federation of Austrian Industries, the Austrian Trade Union Federation, the Federal Social Welfare Department and the Vienna Board of Education. The measure was launched in 2013 and targets the whole population, though many migrants belong to the group under consideration. There are three major areas of activity: 1) school and vocational training; 2) vocational training for adults; and 3) information and motivation, for which a set of concrete measures has been launched. The implementation of the Vienna 2020 Qualification Plan is constantly evaluated, monitored and updated.

One concrete example of the measures in the Vienna 2020 Qualification Plan is "catching up on graduations" for persons without a finished apprenticeship. It has been implemented in Vienna for both employed and unemployed adults. Unskilled workers with concrete professional experience are admitted to these tests. The measure is implemented in co-operation between WAFF and AMS. Besides that, the Chamber of Labour and the Economic Chamber offer counselling for migrants who want to earn a professional degree.

Source: Reeger and Enengel, 2016.

A growing number of migrants is trying to access the Vienna labour market via self-employment. The Vienna Business Agency's service Migrant Enterprises offers counselling and coaching regarding founding a company, financing and concrete funding, in 17 languages and free of charge. The focus is on start-ups and the early stages of the company phase. Migrant Enterprises also acts as the contact point for low-cost office spaces. Self-employment is also a module of the "Start Wien" Coaching programme. Newcomers interested in setting up a business are directly connected with Migrant Enterprises, where they are offered individual counselling. The recent influx of refugees has resulted in adding Arabic and Farsi to the counselling languages.

According to the expert interview, 37% of business owners in Vienna had a migration background in 2012 and it can be assumed that the share is growing, as many recently arrived migrants from the eastern European EU countries engage in one-person companies most of all in the care sector and in construction. Previous studies have shown the sometimes problematic situations of these entrepreneurs such as self-exploitation and weak positions (Reeger and Enengel, 2016), still many choose this path due to the lack of chances in the labour market. About 40-50% of the consultations at Migrant Enterprises per year result in concrete counselling and coaching, with the rest lacking feasibility.

In addition to the AMS services available (see Chapter 3), the Province of Vienna added other labour market integration measures for welfare recipients with the project Job-chance, as well as Equal and Step2Job. The projects offer participants paid employment and support in other matters – training, counselling and job placement. By the end of the project period, the participants are supposed to find permanent employment in the primary labour market. The funding for 2012 amounted to approximately EUR 2 150 000 from the city of Vienna, the AMS, and the European Social Fund. In 2015, the city spent EUR 544 million for this measure, which amounts to 4.3% of the city's total budget.[1]

A measure designed for a specific migrant group, namely undocumented workers, is UNDOK, a contact point and counselling institution. It was established in 2014 by some professional unions, the Chamber of Labour and various non-governmental organisations (NGOs). The aim is to support workers suffering from exploitation by providing individual counselling for free. Moreover, the contact point supports people without residence and/or employment permits in law enforcement and provides information about the contact point and its services as well as social rights (Koppenberg, 2015; UNDOK, 2015; Reeger and Enengel, 2016). Though EU migrants are not the sole target of UNDOK, a billboard campaign at the beginning of the 2015 harvest season on large roads from Hungary, Slovenia and the Slovak Republic to Austria was carried out. In the respective languages, the posters said "Welcome to Austria. Your minimum wage in harvesting is 6 euros". The aim of the campaign was not only to inform seasonal workers but also to raise awareness among employers in agriculture. The German version subsequently reads, "Wage dumping is criminal".[2]

Objective 10. Secure access to adequate housing

The Vienna housing market situation is generally rather tight due to the dynamic population growth of the Vienna urban region. Rents on the private market and prices for owner-occupied flats are increasing and there is a deepening shortage of affordable, decent housing that affects not only migrants, but the whole urban population.

Most migrants settle along the "belt", a broad road along the former city walls bordering the city centre from northwest and southwest, where the larger working-class districts were located and rents are cheaper. The region east of the Danube is only sparsely inhabited by migrants, even less so the more remote but affluent areas of the western and southern districts. New immigrants on average have 40% less living space per capita than native-borns (24 m^2 against Vienna average being 40 m^2). Also people who migrate late to Vienna and concluded their education in Austria generally pay on average EUR 2/m^2 more on living space than native-borns (Stadt Wien, 2017). With regard to homeless services provided by the city of Vienna, in 2012 three in four clients were Austrian citizens, 5.7% nationals of other EU member states, and 18.5% were third-country nationals.

Municipal social housing is managed by "Wiener Wohnen", a housing agency associated with the city of Vienna. Social housing consists of approximately 220 000 municipal flats. This makes up 23.6% of the housing stock. A further 220 000 municipal flats are subsidised and owned by a limited profit housing association. Consequently about 43.4% of total housing stock is socially bound (see Table 7.1).

Table 7.1. Housing statistics for Vienna, 2016

	Flat	Percent	
Flats (principal residence)	901 900	100%	
House ownership	58 000	6.4%	
Condominium flats	113 000	12.5%	
Rental flats (total)	691 000	76.6%	
...Municipal flats (owned by the city of Vienna)	213 000	23.6%	43.4% permanently socially bound
...Subsidised flats (owned by limited-profit housing associations)	179 000	19.8%	
...Private rental flats	299 000	33.2%	
Others	406 000	45.0%	

Source: Statistik Austria, Wohnen 2016, Zahlen, Daten und Indikatoren der Wohnstatistik, Wien 2017.

Until 2006, foreign citizens could not access social housing services. This policy had the unintended implication that the migrant population is not concentrated in areas where social housing was built but on the private rental market in areas just outside the city centre. The highest concentration of migrants was living in areas where rents were lower, with non-renovated houses. The municipality subsidised the renewal of many houses in neighbourhoods with a high concentration of migrants, which favoured gentrification of some of those areas. Since 2006, access to social housing has been extended to migrants – irrespective of (country of) origin – but upon the requirement that the person has lived for five years in Austria and two years continuously at the same address in Vienna. Furthermore, depending on their income, tenants may receive housing subsidies. These are provided on an individual basis and can be used not only in social housing, but also for private rental flats. Access to social housing, renovation subsidies and migrants' capacity to pay higher rents contributed to decreasing segregation (OECD questionnaire, 2017).

This rule explains why foreign groups score low (Figure 7.1) in access to subsidised housing offered by housing associations (OECD questionnaire, 2017). Added to that, the majority of migrants have limited access to owner-occupied housing due to financial constraints on the one hand, and reasons related to the temporality of their migration on the other (e. g. mobile EU citizens, students). This leaves the private rental market, which is accessible immediately.

The private rental market is the most common housing option for migrants, as this is the only feasible option, at least at the beginning of the stay. Almost 50% of migrants from Turkey reside in municipality-owned social housing, the highest share across all groups. Owned homes are an option for Austrian born persons (24.4%) and immigrants from EU-15 (23.4%), who are better off in financial terms compared to other EU migrants and third-country nationals.

According to the information provided by the representatives of the city of Vienna (OECD questionnaire, 2017), more than 75% of main residence dwellings in Vienna are rental, which is clearly above the share of the rest of Austria (about 30%), where privately owned housing prevails. The city of Vienna stated no concrete policies, project or initiatives in the field of housing specifically for migrants, except for refugees, which have been described in Chapter 3.

Figure 7.1. Type of accommodation by place of birth in Vienna, 2013

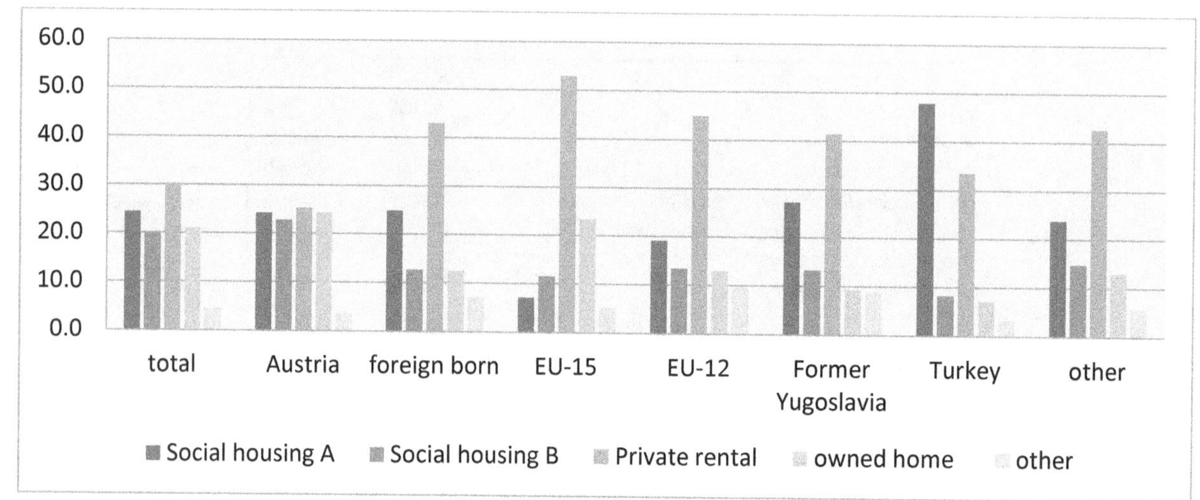

Note: Social housing A = Flats owned by the municipality; Social housing B = Subsidised co-operative flats; Other: Company flats, relatives etc.
Source: Author, based on OECD questionnaire filled in by the city of Vienna and Microcensus 2013.

Homelessness is of growing relevance. According to current estimates (FSW), there are about 10 000 homeless persons in Vienna, among them more than 1 200 "rough sleepers", people sleeping outside and eventually looking for a place in a shelter. NGOs (Zweite Gruft, Vinziport) state higher numbers – up to 3 000 rough sleepers including those in and out of emergency shelters. Rough sleepers are EU migrants not entitled to social benefits coming from central and eastern Europe. They can be discerned into two groups: 1) persons who have worked for some years in Austria, but due to missing or fragmentary insurance and/or registration periods cannot access the welfare system; and 2) persons fleeing from poverty, homelessness and persecution in the countries of origin, and lack prior employment in Vienna. According to the ambulatory division of the Viennese Assistance to the Homeless (Verban Wiener Wohnungslosenhilfe) that provides emergency shelters, soup kitchens and street work, the presence of homeless persons who are non-eligible for benefits according to the Vienna Social Welfare Act has been growing ever since the EU accession round of 2004 (Chwistek, 2013: 1).

Accommodation options for the homeless in Vienna are rather limited. Only in the time period from November to April are they allowed to enter emergency shelters during the night (financed by the FSW). Additionally, two private institutions financed by donations ("Zweite Gruft" run by Caritas and the emergency shelter of the Vinzenzgemeinschaft) offer possibilities for staying overnight, also during the summer period.

Objective 11. Provide social welfare measures that are aligned with migrant inclusion

Generally speaking, the Austrian welfare regime is based on a corporatist model and a stable social partnership between employers, employees and the state. It is based on contributions and eligibility is linked to the previous activity of the individual. Social security covers sickness, invalidity, maternity, unemployment, old age, nursing care and social need. Social insurance is compulsory for both self-employed and gainfully employed persons with insured persons being legally entitled to benefits. Funding comes from income-related insurance contributions (from employees and employers) and state support (taxes). The principle of solidarity ensures that those with higher incomes – who therefore pay higher social insurance contributions – help to fund benefits for those with lower incomes (Reeger and Enengel, 2016).

The means-tested minimum income (City of Vienna, 2012) scheme (Bedarfsorientierte Mindestsicherung, BMS) is a welfare benefit[3] based on an agreement between the national level and the federal provinces that sets out key aspects to be transposed into laws on the federal-provincial level (Reeger and Enengel, 2016). It traditionally covers the provision of basic material needs. It is a combination of needs-based income (cash benefit), health insurance (e-card), subsidy for housing costs, rent allowance (if the rent is higher than the subsidy), a mobility pass. According to the Federal Ministry of Social Affairs (2014):

> *BMS comprises benefits to ensure people's means of subsistence and housing needs, and to afford protection in case of sickness, pregnancy and childbirth. A flat-rate benefit (= minimum standard), it is designed to ensure coverage for recurring expenses on food, clothing, personal hygiene, household effects, heating and electricity, as well as on personal needs to enable claimants to enjoy appropriate social and cultural participation.*

The **Viennese model of BMS** transformed in September 2010 the needs-based minimum basic income into a measure aimed at bringing as many people of working age as possible into the labour market. Vienna additionally provides active support for job seeking and involves social counselling. Persons without health insurance are granted access to the healthcare system. This measure is accessible to all Austrian citizens or persons with an equal status who permanently live in Vienna and who have an income lower than the minimum standard.[4] EU migrants have a right to claim BMS according to the EU's non-discrimination rules, however certain conditions apply according to EU directives which primarily require employment status. The amounts of the minimum benefits are set by the city of Vienna. In 2016, single persons/single parents received up to EUR 838, couples EUR 628 per person and for each child EUR 226 (Stadt Wien, n.d.b)

In 2015, Vienna had 180 646 recipients of BMS, 12.9% more than in 2014. The number of Austrian recipients decreased from 69% in 2011 to 57% in 2015, while migrant groups receiving BMS increased. Most recipients come from Turkey, Serbia, Syria, Afghanistan, Poland, Romania, Russia and Bulgaria. Only 10% of the recipients get the full amount of BMS; more than three-quarters receive so-called supplementary benefits, because their income, unemployment benefit or sustenance is too low. In Vienna, BMS is denied if people who are able to work do not actively engage in finding a job.

Health insurance covers all persons in employment and their family members, unemployed persons who receive benefits, retirees, welfare beneficiaries, refugees and asylum seekers are also covered. According to the Federal Ministry of Health and Women's Affairs, compulsory health insurance covers 99.9% of the population (ICMPD, 2016: 53).

Irregular migrants do not benefit from the welfare system and are not subject to official healthcare. AMBER-MED is an NGO offering healthcare for uninsured persons regardless of origin. Being a joint effort of the Diakonie Austria and the Red Cross, AMBER-MED is largely funded by private donations together with the Vienna Health Insurance Fund (FSW) and the Federal Ministry of Health. AMBER-MED operates free and anonymously. For EU migrants from Romania and Bulgaria, there are consultation hours every week in the respective languages (Reeger and Enengel, 2016).

> **Box 7.2. Healthcare measure focusing on migrants**
>
> A rare example for a healthcare measure directly focusing on migrants is the NGO Volkshilfe's (Peoples' Aid) who offers MiMi (health with migrants for migrants), an intercultural health programme funded by BMEIA and the Health Insurance Fund. Launched in 2012, well-established migrants are trained as health guides (more than 50 hours of training) to inform other migrants about topics related to healthcare. These health guides subsequently offer information events in migrant communities (Reeger and Enengel, 2016).
>
> For more information, see www.volkshilfe-wien.at.

In co-operation with hospitals (with religious belonging), the NGO Caritas runs a mobile medical office "Louise-Bus" that provides medical support for homeless persons (see Reeger and Enengel, 2016). From Monday to Friday, the Louise-Bus stops at set places in Vienna for several hours, where doctors and volunteer helpers look after patients.

The ESRA Psychosocial Centre offers comprehensive professional help to people who have been traumatised because of persecution, torture, migration, abuse, disasters or other serious events. It provides a variety of services in the fields of medicine, psychiatry, psychotherapy, psychology, care and social work with a view to helping people to deal with the psychological consequences of traumatic events and to provide them with a new perspective. It is funded by the FSW and the national level. Another NGO, HEMAYAT, provides interpreter-mediated psychotherapy, psychological consulting and medical support for survivors of war and torture. Funding comes from FSW, MA 17, BMI and other sources (see www.hemayat.org). ESRA and HEMAYAT offer outreach services in the refugee facilities, including counselling and training for the on-site staff.

Objective 12. Establish education responses to address segregation and provide equitable paths to professional growth

Education is the basis for economic integration and social societal participation. It significantly increases employability and strengthens cultural possibility to become active in democratic society (Stadt Wien, 2014).

While generally educational attainment increases for all, educational gaps in terms of weaker educational performance is a reality in Vienna. Particularly in more recent years Vienna has experienced increased immigration from highly qualified migrants with a university degree. Some 32% of migrants from a third country have studied and 34% of EU27/EFTA states come with a university degree (OECD questionnaire, 2017).

Native-born children with migrant parents who are educated in Austria obtain similar forms of higher education, compared to their native-born peers. Yet, the numbers for those only completing compulsory education are 7% higher for children with migration background educated in Austria. Overall, foreign-born groups educated abroad have lower educational attainment results, counting higher percentages of persons without a degree and larger low-qualification shares (Stadt Wien, 2017).

While the substantial frames for education policies are decided on the federal level, the city itself can still give an impetus and contribute by providing specific activities. Integration is measured based on the conception that all people living in Vienna should have the same access to education and can - independent of their legal and social status - reach similar competencies (Stadt Wien, 2014). The following approaches demonstrate how the city engages in education.

Measures for children of, and before, mandatory school age

In 2009, the national and the federal-provincial governments agreed on the implementation of one year of compulsory attendance in kindergarten for all children registered in Austria (Reeger and Enengel, 2016). The aim is to promote integration and language skills of all children (with and without a migration background). Attendance at public childcare facilities has been free of charge since then, with children staying for at least 16-20 hours per week. Both the national and the federal-provincial level provide funding and the measure has been prolonged for another three years. The federal provinces are responsible for the concrete implementation of this measure of early linguistic assistance. In Vienna, multi-professional and multi-lingual teams have been mobilised in schools and learning materials have been expanded.

Regarding school enrolment, the Vienna Board of Education has recently established transitional classes with the aim of harmonising the education level reached in the country of origin with Austrian standards in order to enable migrant children to continue studies within the Austrian system (OECD questionnaire, 2017). Generally, however, migrant children in compulsory schools are placed in regular classes together with native children and are educated together and not apart. To adjust for special needs of migrant children several accompanying actions have been implemented: the number of teachers in classes has been increased ("team teaching"), language support and intercultural learning was introduced. As a reaction to the recent influx of refugee children, some schools employ teachers who are refugees themselves on an honorary basis in order to support refugee children.

Furthermore, Vienna provides children and young people who need to improve their German language skills with specific courses in the summer and during the school year (OECD questionnaire, 2017). Summer language courses are on offer for children and young people between 7 and 14 years of age who have problems with the German language. The courses focus on migrant children who arrive in Austria during the school year and on children with German as a mother tongue who (nearly) failed their German class at school. The courses also include sports and leisure activities; they take two weeks and can be attended half-day or full-day.

Kindergartens and schools are also the venues for the project "Mum learns German" that offers language courses at a very basic level for female adults. Concretely, the language training specifically targets mothers with children enrolled in kindergarten or school who have few social contacts and a low educational level (Interface Wien, 2015). This measure is funded by MA 17.

Learning support and German language courses for children between 11 and 14 in the project "Sowieso mehr!" (Anyways More!) by Interface are offered for those who need to improve their German language skills or skills in other school subjects during the school year. Courses are held at out-of-school facilities twice a week for two hours and also during the holidays.

Measures for youth

As a reaction to the inflow of young asylum seekers as of 2015, the project "Start Wien – Youth College" was launched in July 2016 with 1 000 places for asylum seekers, recognised refugees and other migrants beyond compulsory school age (15–21). Led by the Vienna Public Learning Centres (Wiener Volkshochschulen GmbH, VHS) a consortium of nine organisations (e. g. Caritas, Interface) offer this service in two locations in Vienna. The goal is to help young asylum seekers and refugees get ready to enter secondary school or job training via a modular system. The budget amounts to EUR 6 million per year; half of it comes from EC-ESF, the other half from funding by MA 17, AMS Vienna and the FSW. Again, this project is based on the idea of "integration from Day 1", as it can be implemented before the status decision.

A second youth college also is targeted at young migrants (not necessarily refugees), who have newly arrived in Austria and who are older than mandatory school age, who need specific support in the form of language courses, creative and social education, and detailed advice about their educational and professional opportunities (OECD questionnaire, 2017). Interface Vienna and the Vienna Public Learning Centres provide young migrants between 15 and 21 years of age with a package of specific educational measures that is also funded by MA 17, ESF, AMS and BMBF (Federal Ministry of Education). The German language and orientation courses help young migrants in meeting the requirements of the Integration Agreement and aim to support them until they have completed language level B1 to be well prepared for further training and education and the working world. Courses of up to 20 hours per week are held at different times in several districts of Vienna.

The Public Employment Service AMS and the Austrian Federal Economic Chamber WKO have jointly (and in co-operation with the Federal Ministry of Economy and Labour) initiated the project b.mobile that targets primarily young recognised refugees who are interested in an apprenticeship. The goal is to match them with enterprises needing apprentices in all federal provinces. In early 2016, when the project was set up, there were 6 500 young refugees and beneficiaries of subsidiary protection registered as unemployed in Austria, with a clear focus on Vienna. On the other hand there was, and still is, an urgent need for apprentices in the western part of Austria. Interested persons can participate in an assessment of competences (in Arabic, English, French and Farsi); the matchmaking with enterprises is the task of the Austrian Economic Chambers. On the level of federal provinces, apprenticeship coaches take care of the refugees in terms of accommodation, but also provide personal and psychological advice, if necessary.

Adult education

In contrast to EU migrants, those from third countries have to sign the "Integration Agreement", which includes the obligation to acquire sufficient German language skills within two years (see Reeger and Enengel, 2016). In order to accomplish this goal, they get financial funding to attend language courses. As EU nationals do not have to sign the Integration Agreement, they also get no public funding from the national level. In Vienna, they get vouchers in case they attend the Start Wien programme. By contrast, third-country nationals, subject to the Integration Agreement, can combine the Start Wien vouchers with vouchers from the national level worth up to EUR 750. The money is only available after the language test has been passed. Vouchers from the city of Vienna are worth EUR 300 for third-country nationals and EUR 150 for EU citizens, and can be used immediately.

In 2012, after many years of promoting German language courses for applicants aspiring to fulfil the Integration Agreement, MA 17 became the official unit in charge of promoting and organising basic education measures for adults in the Federal Province of Vienna and receives federal and EC-ESF funding to accomplish this task (OECD questionnaire, 2017). To be eligible for MA 17 funding, education facilities must be accredited by the Austrian Federal Ministry of Education. The accreditation is based on a comprehensive assessment.

The city of Vienna offers adult migrants a large variety of language courses. Training courses are free of charge for third-country nationals and the maximum group size is ten people. Participants receive individual counselling on training and education issues, as well as accompanying social counselling and extensive documentation. The focus of basic education is not only on acquiring German language skills, but also on further basic skills such as reading, writing, mathematics, information technology, citizenship and preparation for the official Austrian language diploma (ÖSD). People with little or no education are the target group to receive a basic education. In addition to basic education courses, MA 17 and the FSW are also in charge of offering other German language courses to different target groups with a focus on their needs. In 2015 and 2016, the focus was primarily on German language courses and preparation courses for the ÖSD exam for refugees (OECD questionnaire, 2017).

Regarding the integration of migrant women with little or no school education into the labour market, the "Women's college" offers training courses where women can learn German as well as other important basic skills such as mathematics and computer skills. These courses are free of charge and provide babysitting if necessary.

There are many different funding schemes and providers of language courses (Reeger and Enengel, 2016). The city of Vienna had for a long time tried to gather information about "language course players" in order to enhance transparency. Unlike in Germany or Sweden, there is no consistent national system of language training in place. The federal level (BMEIA, Austrian Integration Fund, AMS), provinces and municipalities are all involved, but not consistently, a fact that has been criticised most of all by representatives of federal provinces and among them, Vienna. In Vienna, Start Wien has established a database of all courses and Start Coaching advises migrants which courses fit the individual needs. For asylum seekers, *Bildungsdrehscheibe* has been implemented for a successful placement into all available courses funded by the city.

Key observations: Block 4

- Despite not being directly responsible for labour market matching, the city has identified crucial aspects concerning labour market and employment integration and identified ways to address this in their margin of manoeuvre. One concern is unemployment rates for so-called "NEETs" - young people who are neither in training nor education nor employment. A particularly large share (29%) of them are women from third countries, while native-born women only make up 5%. While the share of NEETs without migration background as well as those of migrants educated abroad decreased, the number of migrants or children of migrant parents increased during the past three years from 17% to 20%. In order to especially target unemployment of (young) people who have not had any schooling the city and other key stakeholders such as the Trade Union and the Public Employment Service have collaboratively set up the "Vienna Qualification Plan". The plan aims to close the gap between low qualified people and a labour market that requires well-qualified staff.

- Social housing is only accessible to foreigners who lived in Austria for at least five years and two years at the same address in Vienna. This limits access to the generally large socially bound housing stock of the city (43.4% of all flats) for migrants who are looking for accommodation on the private rental market. Furthermore, depending on their income, tenants may receive housing subsidies. These are provided on an individual basis and can be used not only in social housing, but also for private rental flats.

- Particularly in more recent years Vienna has experienced increased immigration from highly qualified migrants with a university degree. Some 32% of migrants from a third country have studied and 34% of EU27/EFTA states come with a university degree. Overall however, especially migrants or migrant children who were not educated in Austria have lower educational performance than their counterparts receiving Austrian education. While the substantial frameworks for education policies are decided on the federal level, the city itself gives an important impetus to the other government levels and contributes by providing a large variety of specific activities. For example, transitional classes with the aim of harmonising educational levels from abroad with national levels were established, enabling migrant children to continue their education in the Austrian system. Also, summer classes were introduced and courses for parents of migrant children installed to build their understanding of the educational system and provide them with the needed language skills.

Notes

1. See http://diepresse.com/home/innenpolitik/5069189/Wer-die-Mindestsicherung-bezieht.

2. Refer to www.augustin.or.at.

3. Welfare benefits are distinguished from insurance benefits as they don't require prior payment of contributions and are tax-funded. Benefits are distinguished from universal benefits as the beneficiaries have to explicitly prove their financial need.

4. Eligible persons: Austrian citizens, recognised refugees and persons with subsidiary protection status, EU/EEA citizens and Swiss nationals (under certain conditions), third countries nationals with a permanent leave to remain, or a family member or a residence permit, or a residence permit for permanent residence, granted by another EU state. It targets people with no or very low income, to combat poverty and social exclusion and recently to reintegrate the labour market. The beneficiaries (129 000 recipients in 2011 in Vienna) include school children, pensioners and people who have been unfit to work for over a year, people who are fit for work or temporarily absent from the labour market (childcare), households that have no source of income.

References

Astleithner, F. and A. Hamedinger (2003), "Urban Sustainability as a New Form of Governance: Obstacles and Potentials in the Case of Vienna", *Innovation: The European Journal of Social Science Research* 16: 51-75.

AWZ (n.d. Version 3), "Bildungberatung fuer AsylbewerberInnen in der Gundversorgung Wien", Aus- und Weiterbildungszenturm Wien.

BFA (2016), "Jahresbilanz 2016", Bundesamt fuer Fremdwesen und Asyl.

BFA (2015), "Jahresbilanz 2015", Bundesamt fuer Fremdwesen und Asyl.

Boulant, J., M. Brezzi and P. Veneri (2016), "Income levels and inequality in metropolitan areas: A comparative approach in OECD countries"

BMF (n.d.), "Bundesministerium fuer Finanzen", retrieved September 2017, from Finanzbeziehungen zu Ländern und Gemeinden, www.bmf.gv.at/budget/finanzbeziehungen-zu-laendern-und-gemeinden/finanzbeziehungen-zu-laendern-u-gemeinden.html.

BMI (n.d.), "Bundesministerium fuer Inneres", retrieved September 2017, from Asylbetreuung, www.bmi.gv.at/cms/BMI_Asyl_Betreuung/asylverfahren/start.aspx.

BMI (2014/2015), "Bundesministerium fuer Finanzen", retrieved September 2017, from Budget 2014/2015, www.bmf.gv.at/budget/das-budget/budget-2014-2015.html.

Bundeskanzleramt Osterreich (n.d.), help.gov.at, retrieved from Allgemeines zum Asyl, www.help.gv.at/Portal.Node/hlpd/public/content/321/Seite.3210001.html.

Charbit, C. (2011), "Governance of public policies in decentralised contexts: The multi-level approach", *OECD Regional Development Working Papers*, No. 2011/04, OECD Publishing, Paris, http://dx.doi.org/10.1787/5kg883pkxkhc-en.

Charbit, C. and M. Michalun (2009), "Mind the gaps: Managing Mutual Dependence in Relations among Levels of Government", *OECD Working Papers on Public Governance*, No. 14, OECD Publishing, Paris. doi:10.1787/221253707200

Chwistek, P. (2013), "Obdachlose EU-BürgerInnen und die Wiener Wohnungslosenhilfe", Eine Bestandsaufnahme, Soziales_Kapital 10, Wien.

City of Vienna (2012), "Summary of the Vienna Social Welfare Report 2012", City of Vienna, Municipal Department 24 - Health Care and Social Welfare Planning.

City of Vienna (2014), 3rd Vienna Integration and Diversity Monitor 2011 until 2013, https://www.wien.gv.at/menschen/integration/pdf/monitor-2014.pdf.

City of Vienna (2017),4th Monitoring integration diversity Vienna 2013-2016, https://www.wien.gv.at/menschen/integration/pdf/monitor-2014.pdf.

Eurostat (2016), *Labour Force Survey in the EU, candidate and EFTA countries*, Publications Office of the European Union, Luxembourg.

Fassmann, H. and J. Kohlbacher (2009), "Diversity policy in employment and service provision – Case study: Vienna, Austria", www.eurofound.europa.eu/publications/htmlfiles/ef09171.htm.

Federal Ministry of Social Affairs (ed.) (2014), "Social protection in Austria", Vienna.

Frauenberger, S. (2016), "Integrtaionsmassnehmen fuer Fluechtling ein Wien", Buero der Stadtraetin Sandra Frauenberger.

FSW (ed.) (2017), "Flüchtlinge, Asyl und Grundversorgung", Grafiken und Daten zu Wien, Österreich und der EU, Wien.

Gruber, M. (2012), "Role of municipalities in fostering integration process of people with migration background in Austria", *Migration Letters* 9/3: 263-272.

ICMPD (2017), "City Migration Profile Vienna. Report for the Project "Mediterranean City-to-City Migration Dialogue, Knowledge and Action", Vienna.

Interface Wien (2015), "Mama lernt Deutsch", www.interface-wien.at/3-eltern-kinder/40-mama-lernt-deutsch.

Koppenberg, S. (2015), "Austria. Annual Policy Report 2014", International Organization for Migration (IOM), Vienna.

Kraler, A. (2011), "The case of Austria", in G. Zincone, R. Penninx and M. Borkert (eds.), *Migration Policymaking in Europe: The Dynamics of Actors and Contexts in Past, Present and Future*, Amsterdam University Press, Amsterdam, pp. 21-59.

Kraler, A., J. Edthofer, E. Enzenhofer and B. Perchinig (2014), "Background Report - Inequalities and Multiple Discrimination in Access to Health in Austria", ICMPD and Research Institute of the Red Cross, Vienna.

Marcos Diaz Ramirez & Thomas Liebig & Cécile Thoreau & Paolo Veneri, 2018. "The integration of migrants in OECD regions: A first assessment," OECD Regional Development Working Papers 2018/01, OECD Publishing.

MA 17 (ed.) (2016), "Vienna is Diversity", Vienna.

MA 5 (ed.) (2016), "Subventionsbericht 2015 der Stadt Wien", Wien.

MA 23 (2017), "Wien in Zahlen", Stadt Wien, Magistrat 23 - Wirtschaft, Arbeit und Statistik.

MA 23 (2016), "Business Location Vienna", Stadt Wien, Wien.

migration.gv.at. (n.d.), "Welcome to the Federal Government's official information website on migration to Austria!", retrieved from www.migration.gv.at/en/welcome/?no_cache=1.

OECD (forthcoming), *The Location of Hosted Asylum Seekers in OECD Regions and Cities*, OECD Publishing, Paris.

OECD (2018), *Working Together for Local Integration of Migrants and Refugees*, OECD Publishing, Paris, https://doi.org/10.1787/9789264085350-en.

OECD (2017), "Migration Policy Database Nr. 13: Who bears the cost of integrating refugees?", January.

OECD (2017a), *International Migration Outlook*, OECD Publishing, Paris, https://doi.org/10.1787/migr_outlook-2017-en.

OECD (2017b), *Multi-level Governance Reforms. Overview of OECD Country Experiences*, OECD Publishing, Paris, https://doi.org/10.1787/9789264272866-en.

OECD (2017c), *The Geography of Firm Dynamics: Measuring Business Demography for Regional Development*, OECD Publishing, Paris, http://dx.doi.org/10.1787/9789264286764-en.

OECD (2017), "How's life in Austria?", in How's Life? 2017: Measuring Well-being, OECD Publishing, Paris, https://doi.org/10.1787/how_life-2017-11-en.

OECD (2016a), "Regional Well-Being", *OECD Countries*, retrieved September 2017, www.oecdregionalwellbeing.org/.

OECD (2016b), Making Integration Work: Refugees and others in need of protection, Making Integration Work, OECD Publishing, Paris, https://doi.org/10.1787/9789264251236-en.

OECD (2009), Closing the Gap for Immigrant Students: Policies, Practice and Performance, OECD Reviews of Migrant Education, OECD Publishing, Paris, https://doi.org/10.1787/9789264075788-en.

OECD (n.d.), "The Vienna Charter: Shaping the future together", Observatory of Public Sector Innovation, www.oecd.org/governance/observatory-public-sector-innovation/innovations/page/theviennachartershapingthefuturetogether.htm#tab_description (accessed 10 April 2018).

Reeger, U. and M. L. Enengel (2016), "Governance approaches to CEE migration in central domains in Austria: Vienna, Linz and the national level", *IMAGINATION Working Paper*, www.eur.nl/fileadmin/ASSETS/fsw/Bestuurskunde/onderzoek/imagination/Austria_WP3.pdf.

Reeger, U. and M. L. Enengel (2015), "Urban implications of CEE migration in Austrian urban regions", *IMAGINATION Working Paper*, www.eur.nl/fileadmin/ASSETS/fsw/Bestuurskunde/onderzoek/imagination/WP2_Austria_UIR.pdf.

Stadt Wien (2017), "4. Wiener Integrtaions- & Diversitaetsmonitor", Wien: Stadt Wien, Magistratsabteilung 17 - Integration und Diversitaet.

Stadt Wien (2015), "Rechnungsabschluss der Stadt Wien", www.wien.gv.at/finanzen/budget/ra15/index.htm, retrieved September 2017.

Stadt Wien (2015c), "MC2CM - city network to promote urban migration and integration policies", www.wien.gv.at/english/social/integration/basic-work/networks/mc2cm.html.

Stadt Wien (2014), "3. Wiener Integrtaions- & Diversitaetsmonitor", Wien: Stadt Wien, Magistratsabteilung 17 - Integration und Diversitaet.

Stadt Wien (2006), "Integration im Öffentlichen Raum", Werkstadtbericht. Magistratsabteilung 18 Stadtentwicklung und Stadtplanung.

Stadt Wien (n.d.), "Migra-Bil - Basiskurs und Workshops", www.wien.gv.at/menschen/integration/projektarbeit/migra-bil.html.

Stadt Wien (n.d.b), "Mindestsicherung", www.wien.gv.at/gesundheit/leistungen/mindestsicherung/.

Stadt Wien (n.d.c), "Bezirkspartnerschaften der Stadt Wien", www.wien.gv.at/politik/international/netzwerke/bezirkspartnerschaften.html.

Statistik Austria (2016), "Arbeitsmarkt Daten", www.statistik.at/web_de/statistiken/menschen_und_gesellschaft/arbeitsmarkt/index.html.

Statistik Austria (2015), "Micozensua", www.statistik.at/web_de/services/mikrodaten_fuer_forschung_und_lehre/datenangebot/standardisierte_datensaetze_sds/index.html#index3

Stanzl, P. and K. Pratscher (2012), "Evaluierung zur Umsetzung der bedarfsorientierten Mindestsicherung", Dokumentation der Jahreskonferenz 2012, in *Österreichisches Komitee Für Soziale Arbeit*, ed. ÖKSA-Jahreskonferenz 2012, Linz.

UNDOK (2015), http://undok.at/.

UNSD (2017), "United Nations Statistics Division", https://unstats.un.org/unsd/demographic/sconcerns/migration/migrmethods.htm#B.

Verwiebe, R., B. Riederer and T. Troger (2014), "Lebensqualität in Wien im 21", Jahrhundert. Endbericht an die Stadt Wien. Vienna.

WAFF (2015a), "Labour market policies in Vienna – priority areas", www.waff.at/html/en/index.aspx?page_url=Arbeitsmarktpolitik&mid=391 (accessed 13 May 2015).

WAFF (2015b), "Vienna's Vocational Training Guarantee", www.waff.at/html/en/index.aspx?page_url=Wiener_Ausbildungsgarantie&mid=369 (accessed 13 May 2015).

Wohnpartner Wien (ed.) (2016), "Jahresbericht Wohnpartner Wien 2015", Wien

Annex A. List of experts interviewed during the OECD site visit, 18-19 January 2017

Stakeholders representing municipal services (in alphabetical order)

- **Nadja Asbaghi-Namin**, Refugee expert, Vienna Social Fund (FSW)
- **Johannes Gielge**, Head of Unit Research Urban Planning, Municipal Department 18 (MA 18) - Urban Development and Planning
- **Karin König**, Legal Expert for Human Rights, Municipal Department 17 (MA 17) – Integration and Diversity
- **Theodora Manolakos**, Research and Monitoring, Municipal Department 17 (MA 17) – Integration and Diversity
- **Christine Petioky**, Co-ordinator and international networks, Vienna Social Fund (FSW)
- **Thomas Trattner**, Head of Department, Vienna Social Fund (FSW)
- **Edith Waltner**, Municipal Department 23 (MA 23) - Economic Affairs, Labour and Statistics
- **Judith Wiesinger**, Social Reporting, Municipal Department 24 (MA 24) – Health Care and Social Welfare Planning

Stakeholders representing other public and private actors (in alphabetical order)

- **Ursula Adam**, Head of the Central Office, Vienna Employment Promotion Fund
- **Robert Dempfer**, Head of the Staff Unit for Social Policy, Austrian Red Cross Austria
- **Petra Draxl**, Regional Managing Director Vienna, Public Employment Service Austria
- **Heinz Fassmann**, Head of the Independent Expert Council for Integration at the Federal Ministry of Europe, Integration and Foreign Affairs
- **Emanuela Hanes**, Office on Social Cohesion and Demographic Change, The Austrian Association of Cities and Towns
- **Anny Knapp**, Chair of the Asylum Coordination Austria
- **Susanne Knasmüller**, Head of the Integration Coordination Department at the Federal Ministry of Europe, Integration and Foreign Affairs
- **Margit Kreuzhuber**, Migration and Integration Officer, Austrian Federal Economic Chamber
- **Bernhard Perchinig**, Senior Research Officer, ICMPD
- **Tülay Tuncel**, Project Co-ordinator, Vienna Business Agency, Migrant Enterprises
- **Josef Wallner**, Head of the Department for Labour Market and Integration, Chamber of Labour Vienna

Annex B. Overview of integration concepts and regulations at national and city level

Regarding the history of migrant integration as elaborated on by the representatives of the city of Vienna in the OECD questionnaire, the city established a "Migrants Fund" (Zuwanderer-Fonds) in 1971 with the aim of supporting both internal and international labour migrants (from the former Yugoslavia and Turkey) by *inter alia* providing cheap housing for their first year of stay.

Following the growing influx of migrants due to the break-up of Yugoslavia and the geopolitical changes in Europe since 1989, the city of Vienna decided to establish an institution targeted directly at the integration of international migrants. In 1992, the "Funds for Integration", was founded as one of the first urban institutions in Europe dedicated to the integration of migrants. The Fund was governed by the mayor of Vienna, and included representatives of both the governing and opposition parties. It soon became a major actor in the field of integration by providing migration-related counselling with regard to legal and social issues, language courses, programmes for children to prepare for school and special programmes in the field of healthcare.

In 1996, the integration agenda moved to a higher political level, and an Executive City Councillor for Integration was appointed. Given the growing relevance of migration in the political debates, the city decided to dissolve the Funds for Integration in 2004 and to establish the Municipal Department for Integration and Diversity (MA 17), which took over the duties of the Funds for Integration and incorporated most of its staff.

With the foundation of MA 17, integration and diversity issues were embedded into the regular city administration. The decision to install a stand-alone municipal department solely dealing with integration and diversity represents a paradigm shift with diversity being a central issue seen as a benefit for the city and this mainstreaming approach generally aiming at the entire Vienna population.

Annex C. Division of competencies between levels of government

Policy area	National government	Province/Municipality Vienna
Asylum seekers and refugees	Aliens Law, Law on Settlement and Residence, Asylum Legislation (Ministry of Interior. BMI)	Implementation of Aliens Law, the law on residence and settlement, asylum law ("mittelbare Bundesverwaltung")
	Initial reception	Allocation of asylum seekers negotiated with the federal government "§15 A-Agreements"
	Allocation of asylum seekers negotiated with provinces "§15 A-Agreements"	Basic assistance - Funding is divided between the federal level and the federal provinces at the ratio of 60:40.
	Basic assistance - Funding is divided between the federal level and the federal provinces at the ratio of 60:40.	Organising accommodation and distribution of basic welfare support
	The national agency BFA (Bundesamt für Fremdenwesen und Asyl) subjected to the BM.I is responsible for Austria for processing and decision on asylum application	Provide special accommodation for vulnerable groups (including unaccompanied minors)
		Support unaccompanied minors (custody)
		Early integration opportunities (Start Wien), i.e. organising language and integration courses for asylum seekers
Education	Design of the education system, supervision of higher education system	Partial design of education system
		Preschool and primary education (City Councils)
		Transitional- and summer classes for newcomers to integrate into Austria's school system
Language learning	Provide migrants and refugees with grants for language classes: people from third countries have to sign the "Integration Agreement", which includes the obligation to acquire sufficient German language skills within two years	Provision and organisation of language courses through various offers (*inter alia* with EU funding), MA 17, preparation = for the Austrian Language Diploma (ÖSD) exam for refugees, special courses for vulnerable groups and with different foci (i.e. women)
	Funding of preschool linguistic assistance	Funding and implementation of preschool linguistic assistance
Vocational training policy	Funding of offers such as b.mobile	Asylum seekers, recognised refugees and other migrants beyond compulsory school age (15–21), such as through Interface Vienna and the Vienna Public Learning Centres, "Women's college", Start Wien – Youth College and other college offers
		Measures in Vienna 2020 Qualification Plan, such as "catching up on graduations"
Social policy	BMS is based on an agreement with provinces	Social services administration Vienna model of BMS (EUR 838, couples EUR 628 per person and for each child EUR 226)
	Funding and design of measures for social inclusion	Funding and design of measures for social inclusion

Policy area	National government	Province/Municipality Vienna
		Youth policies
		Co-ordination of integration matters on the provincial level
Employment	Labour migration regulation "Red-White-Red Card", Foreigners' Employment Act[1] (Federal Ministry of Labour and Social Affairs , BMASK)	Contact Point for the Recognition and Assessment of Qualifications Obtained Abroad (AST)
	Recognition of qualifications obtained abroad	The Vienna model of BMS foresees that people are excluded who are not trying to get a job
	The means-tested minimum income scheme (Bedarfsorientierte Mindestsicherung BMS) (welfare benefit) is based on an agreement between the national level and the federal provinces that sets out key aspects to be transposed into laws on the federal-provincial level	Local measures for access to and participation in the labour market
		Training and stimulation of entrepreneurship as a module of Start Wien
	Service and programmes offered by the Public Employment Service Austria (AMS)	Dialogue for co-operation between the public authorities and business
Housing	Provides funding for building social housing	Building and management of social housing and municipal land, in collaboration with private companies
		Allocation of quota (social housing) and municipal subsidies
Spatial planning		Urban and regional planning
Public health	Initial medical check-up for newly arrived	Initial medical check-up for newly arrived
	Health insurance covers all persons in employment and their family members, unemployed persons who receive benefits, retirees, welfare beneficiaries, refugees and asylum seekers	Healthcare for migrants
Public administration	Reviewing resident permits and visas	Local access to public services
Public order and safety	National Security Framework	Maintaining public order in the municipality and local police
Economic development	National Economic Strategy	Local/Regional Economic Strategy

Note: 1. The Foreigners' Employment Act targets all foreign nationals except for *inter alia* recognised refugees, those under subsidiary protection, EU/EEA citizens, diplomats and Swiss citizens.
Source: OECD questionnaire completed by the city of Vienna.

ORGANISATION FOR ECONOMIC CO-OPERATION AND DEVELOPMENT

The OECD is a unique forum where governments work together to address the economic, social and environmental challenges of globalisation. The OECD is also at the forefront of efforts to understand and to help governments respond to new developments and concerns, such as corporate governance, the information economy and the challenges of an ageing population. The Organisation provides a setting where governments can compare policy experiences, seek answers to common problems, identify good practice and work to co-ordinate domestic and international policies.

The OECD member countries are: Australia, Austria, Belgium, Canada, Chile, the Czech Republic, Denmark, Estonia, Finland, France, Germany, Greece, Hungary, Iceland, Ireland, Israel, Italy, Japan, Korea, Latvia, Lithuania, Luxembourg, Mexico, the Netherlands, New Zealand, Norway, Poland, Portugal, the Slovak Republic, Slovenia, Spain, Sweden, Switzerland, Turkey, the United Kingdom and the United States. The European Union takes part in the work of the OECD.

OECD Publishing disseminates widely the results of the Organisation's statistics gathering and research on economic, social and environmental issues, as well as the conventions, guidelines and standards agreed by its members.

OECD PUBLISHING, 2, rue André-Pascal, 75775 PARIS CEDEX 16
(85 2018 16 1 P) ISBN 978-92-64-30413-0 – 2018